From a Shepherd's
H·E·A·R·T

From a Shepherd's
H·E·A·R·T

Things I want my flock to know

EDWIN F. WHITE

COVENANT
PUBLISHING

International Standard Book Number 1-892435-00-4

Contents

Introduction   *9*

1 Touch One Another in Christian Love   *11*

2 Be Kind to One Another   *21*

3 Be Subject to One Another   *29*

4 Submit to Others Because You Fear Christ   *37*

5 Accept One Another   *45*

6 Love One Another   *53*

7 Live in Harmony with One Another   *61*

8 Agree with One Another   *69*

9 Serve One Another   *77*

10 Resolve Anger Quickly   *87*

11 Be Humble toward One Another   *95*

12 Christian Freedom Is Mature and Responsible   *105*

13 Build Up One Another   *113*

Introduction

I have now served one church for twenty-nine years as its pulpit minister. I also serve the church as one of its shepherds or elders. Although possible, it is unlikely that I will have twenty-nine more years of ministry. I am on shorter notice now. If I had but one more year to love and lead my flock, now spread over all the earth, I would spend the time sharing the truths of this little book. These discoveries were born of experience, refined in the fire of battle against hostile forces that fight against the church, and hammered into existence on the anvil of pain and privation associated with the task of promoting peace and joy among believers.

The all-consuming thought of this book is that Christians cannot live in isolation. Just as a tree draws life from the soil, so Christians draw life from one another. We cannot be glorious or resplendent in our own might or light.

My purpose in writing is to help God's people discover the joy and power of watching for others. The greatest in the Kingdom of God are those who become servants of all. We are our brother's keepers. Glorious joy comes to every Christian who understands that Christianity is a commodity the more of which we export, the more we shall always have remaining.

This book is a companion to my earlier work, *A Sense of Presence*. That book focused attention on the Christian's relationship with God. Its purpose was to help believers become more aware of God and in that awareness to love him above all. This book concentrates on our need to love and serve one another. Aware that the two most important commands of the Bible are to love God and others, I offer this book as a companion to the former work, praying that it will help believers everywhere attain the joy that comes only through selfless love and service to God and men.

You will sometimes find me transparent and a bit vulnerable. I don't mind. Much of what I know about serving God and his people I learned with embarrassment and great difficulty. If it seems at times that I have cut my wrists and am bleeding on the paper, I can only say that my sincere prayer is that these words from a shepherd's heart—things I want my flock to know—will make you a blessing to God and others.

"They do not love that
do not show their love."
—Shakespeare

Number 1

Touch One Another in Christian Love

The first twenty-two years of my ministry with the church in Phoenix found us located in the inner city. Several years ago the church relocated and is now in one of the city's upscale neighborhoods. While in the inner city it was common for street people to walk into our assemblies on Sunday morning. After an initial visit, many of our homeless visitors stopped by the office during the following week. I became well acquainted with several of them. Some were clean. Others were shabby and dirty. Some were rational. Others were irrational. Some needed food, clothing, and shelter. Others needed only to sit, talk, and pray. Some were humorous, talkative, and amusing. Others were sad, broken, desperate, and disturbed. Some managed to improve their lives. Others slipped deeper into the dark abyss of alcohol and drugs. Several died of natural causes. Some were murdered.

Maria Rook was the most memorable of them all. Maria immigrated to America from Germany with her mother when she was a teenager. Now, in her fifties, without family or any means of support, Maria lived on the streets. Although Maria sometimes heard voices and responded to them with great energy and lively gestures, she was harmless and kind. She came by the church office two or three time a week for several years.

Maria ventured forth through an open door only when invited. Upon entering she always bowed, and in a pronounced German accent said, "God bless you, Pastor." I often explained to Maria that in my theological tradition and understanding preachers are not pastors unless they also serve as elders or shepherds. Since I was not an elder at that time, I suggested that she call me by my name, Edwin. One day as she left the office, Maria bowed, backed out the door and said, "God bless you, Pastor."

I answered quickly, "Maria, call me Edwin. Remember that I am not a pastor."

"Yes, I know," she said.

"Thank you, Pastor."

"Thank you, Pastor."

Maria was later bludgeoned to death on a Phoenix street. I miss her. She may have been hopeless and helpless—a beggar—but I will always remember her kindness, humor, and humility.

Another unforgettable street person walked into one of our Sunday morning services. I could not help noticing that he was dirty, smelly, and shabby. His bearded face was filthy, and his clothes were tattered and seedy. His imposing size and powerful physique made him seem ominous and dangerous. My routine of shaking hands and greeting people as they leave the building meant that I would have to touch my squalid guest. When I reached out to shake his hand, he placed his two hands under my armpits and lifted me off the floor as easily as you would lift a feather. I struggled to get loose, but it was impossible. My mind was filled with questions. What does he intend to do? Does he intend to do me bodily harm? Is he angry? There I was, helpless, suspended between heaven and earth, saying to myself, "If he strikes me on one cheek will I make the other available also?" "Do I have a choice?" Suddenly, he pulled our faces together. Never had I smelled such foul breath. With our noses less than an inch apart, he blurted out, "Preacher, that was a helluva sermon, and the Bible says that I should greet you with a holy kiss." He then proceeded, in full view of the whole church, to smack me three times, once on the forehead, and once on each side of my face. The deed done, he loosened his hold on me with the same gusto he used to launch me at the first, and then walked quickly away.

After the shock wore off, I saw the humor in it all, and began to think of the whole incident as one of the most amusing episodes of my life. The event also motivated me to take a closer look at what the scriptures call the "holy kiss." I came to the conclusion that we need to take more seriously the command to touch one another in Christian love.

The Kiss Of Peace

The command to "greet one another with a holy kiss" occurs five times in the New Testament (Romans 16:16; 1 Corinthians 16:20; 2 Corinthians 13:12; 1 Thessalonians 5:26; 1 Peter 5:14). I am impressed that the demand to touch one another in Christian love, repeated five times by two apostles—Paul and Peter—is more relevant than most think. When is the last time you heard a sermon on the command to greet one another with a "holy kiss?" Considering that this command is so oft repeated how can we justify our lack of interest?

Why did the lovely custom of kissing pass from the church's life? We know from ancient writers that the early Christians gave the kiss at the end of prayers and just before the congregation ate the Lord's Supper, as a sign or symbol that those who gathered for worship were joined in perfect love. Is the modern church in less need of a symbol of love and unity than the first century church?

Some suggest that the custom of greeting with a kiss died because it was subject to misuse and abuse. The betrayal kiss Judas gave Jesus unquestionably abused a lovely custom. Also, there was the danger that close physical contact between men and women might elevate feelings of lust and fleshly desire. Others feel that the custom of greeting with a kiss passed because it left the church open to heathen slanders of immorality and perversion. Some feel that the custom of kissing ceased because the church became less a fellowship than a large corporate body. When the small house churches merged to make large congregations in central locations, the church lost its intimacy. With the loss of intimacy came the loss of the custom of greeting with a kiss. When churches grew large they became a collection of strangers or, at best, a group of casual acquaintances. Understandably, not much kissing takes place among strangers and mere acquaintances.

The Influence of Culture

My feeling is that the custom of kissing passed from the church's life primarily because of cultural changes. We now greet one another by saying "hello," or by shaking hands. Occasionally, we greet one another by hugging. We often greet others by asking, "How are you doing?" Sometimes we inquire about family members. Are these new ways of greeting acceptable to God? Yes, if we can see beyond the forms to their function and purpose. Clearly, the command to greet one another with a kiss had as its purpose to make of us a group of people who love one another as family in Christ. The important thing is not that we kiss, although kissing is acceptable among family members, but that we find some expression that will expedite the feeling of family love in the church.

Sadly, many of us do not greet others with any warmth or feeling. Our greetings are hollow and empty. To greet others with the question, "How are you?" when we don't care or really want to know is also hypocritical.

Who can deny that the churches often become a collection of strangers or, at best, casual acquaintances? This church age needs nothing more than for Christians everywhere to touch, tenderly and lovingly, the lives of others.

The Power of A Tender Touch

Who of us has not been raised from the pit of depression and despair by the tender touch of someone who cared? The Ephesian elders consoled themselves, and Paul, when they embraced and kissed him (Acts 20:37), and the prodigal son of Luke 15 was rescued by his father's kiss.

I do not have a single childhood memory of my father embracing me or kissing me. I don't remember him ever saying,

"I love you." While he was always a friend and protector, my father's model of parenting was that of a stern disciplinarian. He was sometimes arbitrary and capricious in his decisions. Although my father was never abusive, he was hard and somewhat cold. Consequently, our relationship throughout life was one of mutual respect and esteem, but never one of warmth and intense attachment or sharing.

Fortunately, in the end, I found an earnest, emotional bond with my father. When I received word that Dad was dying, I had just finished delivering a sermon in the coliseum on the campus of Abilene Christian University. My speech for the annual lectures program at Abilene that year was early in the week, which meant that I could relax and enjoy other speakers and friends for the remainder of lectureship. I recall feeling satisfied that my talk was as successful and helpful as I could make it. I was on an emotional high. I stepped from the platform, the final "amen" not yet spoken, only to receive the bad news that Dad was ill and that I needed to call home. I remember being impressed with the unpredictability of life. One moment finds you on a glorious, sunlit mountaintop of joy. The next moment finds you in the valley of shadows and death.

During those several hours of driving from Abilene to my parent's home in Arkansas, I wondered how I would help ease the ordeal of dying for my father. We were not that deeply attached. We were friendly but distant. How could I be of help? I prayed for an answer. The answer came. Upon my arrival at the hospital, my father asked that I not leave him alone. I stayed with Dad day and night for the next week. During those last days we talked and touched. I turned him in his bed frequently, washed him, and spoke of old memories and good times. He voiced his love for me and affirmed his genuine affection in many ways. Then, he died from complications of lung cancer early on Sunday morning.

I was sad. While I didn't feel like attending church services that morning, or singing hymns of joy, I was pleased that my father and I found healing and deep love during his dying days. I now know that it is important for us to begin showing our love for others early. It is impossible to estimate the power of love's embrace. When it comes to showing our love, we must not waste time.

In this age of despair and division there is a desperate need for us to learn how to give the gentle touch of love. By wrapping our arms around one another, kissing one another, holding hands in a prayer circle—by merely touching one another as Christians—we grow in love for one another. For those who say that touching is an artificial way to promote love—that it is an irresponsible and dangerous trick—I can only say that there must be a reason why two apostles—Paul and Peter—gave the plain command for us to "greet one another with a holy kiss," not once, but five times. Something said so often must be important. Are we willing to say that Paul and Peter were tricksters?

Touching Others with Words

We also touch one another with words. I learned this lesson powerfully many years ago while preaching a "protracted meeting" (they called it right; the meeting lasted two full weeks) for a church in the rural South. By the end of the first week I had begun to notice that one half the church always entered by the front door and sat on the north side of the building. The other half always entered the back door and sat on the south side of the church building. What I didn't know was that two men, father and son, who had serious disagreements with one another, each headed a faction in the church. One group sat on one side of the building, while the other group sat on the opposite side. Each group had its entrance and exit doors, which meant that they could assemble on the Lord's Day without speaking to each other.

The arrangement worked well for several years, but for some inexplicable reason during one of our night services, someone either said something across the aisle, or walked out the wrong door, or did something provocative, and a fight such as I had never seen broke out on the front lawn. The scuffle turned into a riotous, tumultuous, old-fashioned donnybrook. I thought the Hatfields and McCoys had found each other again.

I don't know why I jumped in and began pulling people apart, demanding that they cool off. Maybe it was because I was an impetuous teenage preacher. Perhaps I took leave of my better judgment as I rushed in where angels feared to tread. I do recall feeling ashamed at the attempt of Christians to settle a dispute with a fistfight.

The next day the entire church met to discuss the implications of the fight. After two hours rehearsing the events that led to the present bitterness and division, a father and his son repented, embraced each other, and said, "I love you." Every person in the church then confessed sin, repented, and asked for forgiveness.

The last week of the meeting we baptized several that lived in that little town. Many inactive church members began attending again. That meeting remains the only such effort that I have ever preached where the church had more public responses during the week than it had members when we began.

Because two men said three simple but powerful words, "I love you," an entire church found healing. How powerfully we touch each other with words! Who can estimate the healing power of an embrace?

The Touch of Jesus

Jesus knew the power of touch. He used touch to communicate. He taught a wonderful lesson on the need for humility when he touched the dirty feet of his disciples and washed them. He laid hands on the sick. He caressed little children. Likely, He communicated his special love for John the apostle by embracing him often.

Jesus stands in stark contrast to those who adopt the hard ways of today's world. I recall reading somewhere that Lenin so enveloped himself in his revolutionary work and ideas that he lost all capacity for gentleness and human tenderness. During the extended illness and eventual death of his mother-in-law, Lenin's wife stood a constant vigil at her mother's bedside. One night Krupskaya, Lenin's wife, collapsed exhausted into bed. Before going to sleep she asked Lenin, who was writing at a desk, to awaken her if her mother needed help. The next morning Krupskaya found her mother dead. Lenin was still at work, writing his revolutionary ideas. When his wife confronted him, Lenin replied, "You told me to awaken you if your mother needed help. She died. She didn't need your help."

It is possible, even among Christians, for people to involve themselves so in selfish pursuits that they lose their ability to express kindness to others. I am convinced that the greatest evangelistic thrust of our time, and the best opportunity for peace and unity in the churches, will come in a recovery of the kind of compassion that inspired those first-century Christians to "greet one another with a holy kiss."

Tennessee Williams, the American dramatist best remembered for his successful plays, *The Glass Menagerie*, and *A Streetcar Named Desire*, once said, "Devils can be driven out of the heart by the touch of a hand on a hand . . ." (*The Milk Train Doesn't Stop Here Anymore*). I believe that our touching one another in Christian love drives out the fiendish attitudes that divide Christians and destroy their fellowship.

It is therefore imperative that we greet one another, that we touch one another—either with a kiss, hug, handshake or kind words—so that everyone will know of our love for one another.

Questions For Discussion

1. How many scriptures tell us to "greet one another with a holy kiss?" Where are they found in the Bible?

2. Why did the practice of greeting with a kiss pass from church life?

3. Should we greet one another with a kiss today?

4. How much should we allow culture to influence church practice today?

5. Were early churches more intimate than churches today? Why?

6. What can we do to develop more intimacy among Christians?

7. How do we touch others with words?

8. Why did Jesus seek to touch others?

9. How may we enlarge our capacity for feelings of human tenderness?

10. Why is it important that we greet one another with expressions of love?

"Kindness is a language
which the dumb can speak,
the deaf can understand."
—C.N. Bovee

Number 2

Be Kind to One Another

Most people are supportive and friendly, but a few, for whatever their reasons, hold me in disesteem and disfavor. Even those who have an aversion to me, however, all admit that I am cordial and kind. I am pleased to know that others view me as a friendly, genial person. God knows that I came by my reputation with great difficulty.

Several incidents reveal how tumultuous my temperament was in the beginning. When, for example, I was a nineteen-year-old who had just begun to preach, our membership was with an old, established church in the community where we lived, but I did "appointment preaching" for small churches within driving distance of our home. One night, while sitting in the living room of our small apartment, preparing a sermon for my next appointment, someone rang my doorbell several times. When I answered the door, no one was there. Within a few minutes, the doorbell rang a second time. Again, there was no one present when I answered. As I settled down a third time, deeply absorbed in a study of the text for my coming sermon— a sermon on love from 1 Corinthians 13—several loud bangs on the door interrupted my concentration. To my astonishment, no one was there when I opened the door. "Somebody is playing games with me," I said. I became angry. Quickly, I tossed my Bible onto the couch. Grasping the doorknob, I thought, "The moment this character rings my doorbell again I am going to fling open the door, seize him with both hands, and within a flash—the twinkling of an eye—I will make him wish he had never seen this house."

Unfortunately, a deacon from the local church where we had our membership, not knowing the situation, and unaware that a door-knocking prankster was about to meet his doom, decided to pay us a brief visit while the station across the street repaired his car. He rang my doorbell at the wrong time. I flung open the door, grabbing, screaming, and running out into the night. We hit the ground fully ten feet from the front porch. Only after several seconds of fierce punching, choking, shaking, and verbal abuse, was I interrupted by the recurrent pleadings of a voice that suddenly sounded familiar—a voice that entreated repeatedly, "Edwin! Edwin! What did I do? What's wrong? What's wrong?"

My mischievous door-knocking trickster, of course, got away unblemished. Although I tried often to explain my actions to a friendly deacon, he never understood. After all, Christians should never act as I did that night.

Learning From Mistakes

The irony of it all is that the whole disturbing episode took place during a deep, absorbing period of sermon preparation, using as a text Paul's great discourse on love in 1 Corinthians 13. There I was, in the middle of a passage that affirms love as the greatest virtue in the world, preparing a sermon in which I would extol love's glorious attributes when, suddenly, I tossed the text aside and proceeded to hurt someone.

It occurs to me that it is easy for us quote scripture and preach sermons about our obligation to treat people with kindness, while proceeding, simultaneously, to injure someone. I have heard often, for example, someone quote a passage denouncing the sin of gossip and slander, who then proceeded to hurt others by saying the worst possible things in the coarsest possible ways.

My only consolation is the thought that my rash conduct helped teach me how to love. The embarrassment of the moment, and the profound feeling of remorse that followed, compelled me to give more than lip service in sermons to the great principles of 1 Corinthians 13. I now know that love is more seen than spoken.

Although I believe the words, "I love you," are the three most powerful words in any language, and that it is important for others to hear us say them often, I would prefer that others see, by convincing acts of kindness, my no-holds-barred compassion.

It is, of course, not true that we have to choose between speaking our love and proving it by acts of kindness. The most ingratiating person in the world is the one who both affirms his love and proves it by his behavior. Still, if I had to make a choice between someone who speaks often of his love, but is never near when I need a friend, and another who never says, "I love you," but always finds a way to help bear my burdens, I would choose the latter.

There is a great lesson here for the local churches. Imagine, for example, that in your community there are two churches. One is a church committed to a search for truth. It is an old, established church. Owing to its emphasis and longevity, it has done an excellent job of restoring the true doctrines of the New Testament. Imagine that although this church has done a commendable job of setting forth the truth of the gospel, it seems cold and uncaring.

Imagine that the other church is not, nor has it ever been, concerned with the integrity of the biblical text. It is sectarian, misguided, and like a loaded gun in the hands of a child, may prove fatal to life at any moment. Yet, imagine that this church shows kindness and compassion. When there is a need in the community, this church is always there, helping, praying, and offering whatever assistance possible. Strangers who visit their assemblies receive a warm welcome. They are introduced to the congregation. Everyone greets them. Several extend invitations for the visitors to eat lunch with them at the local cafeteria. This church is friendly, kind, and charming. The atmosphere is one of compassion and genuine concern for the other person.

Imagine that you live in this community, and that you know little about the scriptures. Imagine that you suddenly come to the realization that you and your family need to devote more attention to spiritual pursuits. Which church will you choose? The choice is inevitable. You will always choose the church that loves.

Another Embarrassing Story

I learned this lesson with great difficulty and embarrassment. Considering my impulsive, unrestrained, and shameful scene with a deacon at my front door, you will not find the following story surprising. As a young preacher I served a church in a rural community for three years. During those years I hosted a thirty-minute radio program every Sunday morning. One of the local sects presented a similar program that preceded mine. More often than not, I drove to the studio without a planned sermon topic. I knew only that I would take notes on the sermon that preceded mine, and that I would then deliver a point-by-point rebuttal.

In my polemics against the sectarian religious broadcast that preceded mine, I began finding points of disagreement where none existed. I gloried in the knowledge that I was a "defender of the faith." It was of no consequence that I was hard, unloving, and unkind.

Toward the end of my tenure in that community, the cultist preacher retired. Although he had never said a word about my continued personal attacks over the air, he signed off his last program with the comment, "Goodbye, I love you all, even you, Edwin White, but I will no longer be your inspiration. You are through with me."

His words still ring loudly in my ears after all these years. He is now dead. I cannot apologize. I live with the knowledge that I presented truth (I make no apologies for truth) with a spirit, not of love, but of rancor and hostility. My resentment and anger created problems for the precious Church of Christ in that community that may be impossible to overcome. After all these years, that church remains inert while others, including the sect I attacked, continue to live and grow.

In fairness, I must say that some churches do a good job both of conveying truth, and loving others. Such churches are the most potent forces God has on earth for evangelizing the world. Still, many of us need to learn that truth without love is empty. New Testament Christianity is not just belief in right things, but loving conduct. The prophetic religion of Christ is not conviction of the mind only, but overflow of the heart.

Learning to Love in Christ

Because I am now more sympathetic and compassionate, some feel that I have become weak. A Christian friend recently offered the opinion that I was once a "sound preacher." "Now," he said, "you offer only pink fluff."

I feel that my change in attitude owes itself to spiritual growth. Because I have attained a measure of maturity in Christ, it is now possible for me to be kind, even to those whose views are different from mine. For those who may feel that such kindness represents weakness, not strength, I can only express a feeling that my progress in the faith parallels that of John the apostle. Although John was a violent person at first, he became the apostle of love.

As time approached for Jesus' crucifixion, he set out for Jerusalem. He sent messengers on ahead to a Samaritan village to get things ready. When the people there refused to welcome Jesus, John wanted to "call fire down from heaven to destroy them" (Luke 9:54).

Yet, before the end of his life, the apostle who thought about annihilating others for their insensitivity was willing to destroy himself, if necessary, for others. He wrote,

> This is the message you heard from the beginning: We should love one another. Do not be like Cain, who belonged to the evil one and murdered his brother. And why did he murder him? Because his own actions were evil and his brother's were righteous. Do not be surprised, my brothers, if the world hates you. We know that we have passed from death to life, because we love our brothers. Anyone who does not love remains in death. Anyone who hates his

brother is a murderer, and you know that no murderer has eternal life in him. This is how we know what love is: Jesus Christ laid down his life for us. And we ought to lay down our lives for our brothers. If anyone has material possessions and sees his brother in need but has no pity on him, how can the love of God be in him? Dear children, let us not love with words or tongue but with actions and in truth. This then is how we know that we belong to the truth, and how we set our hearts at rest in his presence whenever our hearts condemn us. For God is greater than our hearts, and he knows everything (1 John 3:11-20).

How do we explain John's remarkable change in attitude? What influences played a role in the apostle's transformation from hostility to humanitarianism? The answer is obvious. John's long, intimate life with Christ taught him how to love. One cannot live continually in Christ's presence, as John did, without learning kindness, for Christ talks about the need for us to love even our enemies. Jesus asks that we bless those who curse us, and do good to those who mistreat us. In his great Sermon on the Mount, Jesus asks,

If you love those who love you, what credit is that to you? Even 'sinners' love those who love them. And if you do good to those who are good to you, what credit is that to you? Even 'sinners' do that. And if you lend to those from whom you expect repayment, what credit is that to you? Even 'sinners' lend to 'sinners,' expecting to be repaid in full. But love your enemies, do good to them, and lend to them without expecting to get anything back. Then your reward will be great, and you will be sons of the Most High, because he is kind to the ungrateful and wicked. Be merciful, just as your Father is merciful. (Luke 6:32-36).

Walking With Christ, We Become Like Him

Owing to his daily walk with the resurrected Christ, John became the preeminent lover of men. He wrote more about the necessity of love than any other apostle. He warned that without love it is impossible to be a Christian, not because he grew weak in old age, but because his life—his long experience in the presence of the one who sacrificed everything at Calvary—forced him to see that self-sacrifice is a necessary component of Christ-likeness.

The problem is that the English word "love" is a capacious word with many meanings. For some, it is that gooey feeling experienced by juveniles. There is the kind of love one has for his puppy, ice cream or pizza. There is the Hollywood brand of love that is frivolous and loose. Someone quipped that towels in Hollywood bathrooms read, "His, Hers, and Next."

Love, such as Christ has for the world, knows no races or faces. It leaves no one on the other side of the road, alone, bleeding to death through the wounds of bitterness and discouragement. The love of Christ wishes the highest good for everyone. Above all, the love of Christ is kind.

John, an apostle of fire in the beginning, became the apostle of affection because, along the way, he learned that to be like Christ means kindness to others.

Like John, we must all follow the example of Christ. We must learn to "be kind and compassionate to one another, forgiving each other, just as in Christ God forgave you" (Ephesians 4:32).

Questions for Discussion

1. Are you a kind person? How do you know?

2. What embarrassment has an act of unkindness caused in your life?

3. What are some of the ways we rationalize our acts of unkindness?

4. In what sense is love more seen than spoken?

5. Do we have to choose between speaking our love and proving it? How may we do both?

6. Why is it important for a local church to be friendly? What are some ways the church may show more warmth and friendliness?

7. What does it mean to speak the truth in love?

8. How do we preach truth without causing resentment?

9. Explain why it is impossible to be like Jesus without being kind to others.

10. Explain how the apostle John made a dramatic change from impatience to forbearance.

Number 3

Be Subject to One Another

Adolph Hitler argued in *Mein Kampf* that the surest way to win victory over reason is by terror and force. With his philosophy of applied force, Hitler made for himself a throne of bayonets. He discovered, unfortunately, that a throne of bayonets is dangerous. It isn't in one's self-interest to sit on one.

Those who live by the sword will die by the sword. Violence can beget only violence. One drawn sword always produces another drawn sword to challenge it. Against naked force, naked force is the inevitable defense.

Because it is human nature to meet force with force, any relationship that must be maintained by coercion is doomed. Even if one is strong enough to make others submit to him, they do not submit in heart. They submit only because strength is inadequate to resist further, and the time will come when it will be necessary to subdue them again.

There is a helpful truth here for everyone interested in maintaining peace and unity among Christians. Relationships among believers, whether in the home, church, or work place, will fail if we stubbornly insist on our rights. Love and goodwill cannot prevail when we demand rigorously from others what we fancy they owe us. Peace comes only when we give humbly to others what God says we owe them.

It is not surprising then that Paul established the principle of mutual subjection among believers. He wrote,

> Submit to one another out of reverence for Christ.
>
> Wives, submit to your husbands as to the Lord. For the husband is the head of the wife as Christ is the head of the church, his body, of which he is the Savior. Now as the church submits to Christ, so also wives should submit to their husbands in everything.
>
> Husbands, love your wives, just as Christ loved the church and gave himself up for her *to* make her holy, cleansing her by the washing with water through the word, *and* to present her to himself as a radiant church, without stain or wrinkle or any other blemish, but holy and blameless. In this same way, husbands ought to love their wives as their own bodies. He who loves his wife loves himself. After all, no one ever hated his own body, but he feeds and cares for it, just as Christ does the church—*for* we are members of his body. "For this reason a man will leave his father and mother and be united to his wife, and the two will become one flesh." This is a profound mystery—but I am talking about Christ and the church. However, each one of you also must love his wife as he loves himself, and the wife must respect her husband. Children, obey your parents in the Lord, for this is right. "Honor your father and mother"—which is the first commandment with a promise—"that it may go well with you and that you may enjoy long life on the earth." Fathers, do not exasperate your children; instead, bring them up in the training and instruction of the Lord. Slaves, obey your earthly masters with respect and fear, and with sincerity of heart, just as you would obey Christ. Obey them not only to win their favor when their eye is on you, but like slaves of Christ, doing the will of God from your heart. Serve wholeheartedly, as if you were serving the Lord, not men, *because* you know that the Lord will reward everyone for whatever good he does, whether he is slave or free. And masters treat your slaves in the same way. Do not threaten them, since you know that he who is both their Master and yours is in heaven, and there is no favoritism with him (Ephesians 5:21-6:9).

In other words, the rule of mutual and reciprocal obligation must prevail in the Christian family. The wife is to submit to her husband, but he is to subordinate himself to her in love. As parents, they must love their children, bringing them up in the teaching and discipline of the Lord, but children are to honor and respect their parents. If the household includes slaves, they must be treated with honor and dignity, but slaves must render enthusiastic service, as if they served Christ himself.

Broad Principle

The remarkable thing is that the ethic of mutual subordination has a broader application in the New Testament than just to the relationships of the Christian home. The New Testament calls upon us to practice the principle of submission in all our relationships, whether they are by choice, birth, or historical circumstances. Christians are, for example, to submit themselves to God (James 4:7; Hebrews 12:9), to the civic authorities (Romans 13:1-7), and to outstanding Christians (1 Corinthians 16:16; 1 Peter 5:5). Even the spirits of the prophets are subject to the prophets (1 Corinthians 14:32).

When the principle of mutual obligation prevails, we forbear and forgive one another (Colossians 3:13), consider one another (Hebrews 10:24), spur one another on toward love and good deeds (Hebrews 10:25), are kind to one another (Ephesians 4:32), do not wrong one another (Galatians 5:13), prefer one another (Romans 12:10), live in harmony with one another (Romans 12:16), love one another (Romans 13:8), do not judge one another (Romans 14:13), accept one another (Romans 15:7), encourage one another (1 Thessalonians 5:11), do not slander one another (James 4:11), and show hospitality to one another (1 Peter 4:9).

Objection

The objection offered most frequently to the principle of mutual subjection is that we are free in Christ. Some argue, "As a Christian I am free from the conscience of others. If I must be in subjection to others, then I am not really free."

In response to this objection three things must be said. First, the New Testament warns against the misuse of freedom.

Paul said, "You, my brothers, were called to be free, but do not use your freedom to indulge the sinful nature, rather, serve one another in love" (Galatians 5:13). Peter encourages us to "Live as free men, but do not use your freedom as a cover-up for evil; live as servants of God" (1 Peter 2:16).

Second, while it is true that the Christian has a cherished and precious freedom in Christ, it is also true that Christian freedom and brotherly love cannot be separated. In Romans 14, a chapter that speaks of the Christian's freedom from the conscience of others more clearly than any other, Paul reminds us that Christianity does not consist in eating and drinking what we like, but in "righteousness, peace, and joy," things that are essentially unselfish.

A new age of joy and peace will dawn in the church when we learn that our rights and freedoms are less important than our obligations. Consequently Paul instructs those who are narrow in their opinions and practice not to judge those who are more broad in their thinking, and those who are broad in their application of Christian principles are not to be offensive to those who are more narrow.

Third, it must be said that the practice of subordinating ourselves to others, far from robbing us of our treasured freedom, is the noblest exercise of freedom. In Paul's epistles the verb "subordinate" occurs twenty-three times. When the apostle uses the active of the verb "subordinate," he attributes to God alone the power to subject others, with a person or thing forced unwillingly into submission.

Something entirely different happens when the apostle speaks of the subordination of Christ, husbands, wives, children, masters, slaves, and all Christians. Then he uses middle or passive indicatives, participles or imperatives of the verb "subordinate," and always describes a voluntary submission. Thus any effort to use the New Testament principle of mutual subjection to force a disciple of Christ into any relationship or association in which he must be amenable to others against his will, does violence to the scripture. Subordination is never subjugation. New Testament submission is not the work of a pitiful peon or puppet with a broken will, but of a free child of God who has made a voluntary decision to help others.

When a Christian voluntarily makes himself amenable to others, placing himself at their service, he shows a greater dignity and freedom than the one who remains interested only in himself. The Christian, who insists on having his way, never giving in to others, loses his freedom in the prison of self-will.

The Example of Christ

When we help others by renouncing rights we possess, not only do we display the noblest exercise of true freedom, but also we imitate the Christ who refused to please himself, subordinating himself to others. Paul put it like this:

> We who are strong ought to bear with the failings of the weak and not to please ourselves. Each of us should please his neighbor for his good, to build him up. For even Christ did not please himself but, as it is written: "The insults of those who insult you have fallen on me" (Romans 15:1-3).

Jesus subordinated himself to others in many ways. He subjected himself to God (1 Corinthians 15:28), and to his earthly parents (Luke 2:51). Incredibly, Jesus subjected himself to all men. Our Lord, for example, subordinated himself to us in the manner of his birth. He came as a king, but he was not born as a prince in a palace. He was born like a slave in a stable. The only memorable thing about Jesus' birthplace was that it needed to be deodorized.

Christ's lowly birth was not accidental. It was a deliberate condescension of divinity that humanity might be exalted. A stainless life was born in the manure and filth of this world that we might have a true vision of humility and goodness—a vision that inspires us to live pure lives in an unclean world.

Jesus also subjected himself to us in the manner of his life. He did not please himself when he put on a slave's apron and undertook to wash our dirty feet (John 13:4-5). He came as one who serves, not as one who must be served.

The ultimate subjection of Jesus to us was in his death. Paul said,

Do nothing out of selfish ambition or vain conceit, but in humility consider others better than yourselves. Each of you should look not only to your own interests, but also to the interests of others. Your attitude should be the same as that of Christ Jesus: Who, being in very nature God, did not consider equality with God something to be grasped, but made himself nothing, taking the very nature of a servant, being made in human likeness. And being found in appearance as a man, he humbled himself and became obedient to death—even death on a cross (Philippians 2:3-8).

Clearly, Christ emptied himself of all pride and status when he died for us. Equally clear is Paul's point that we are to have the same mind of humility that Christ had. If Christ submitted to others, how dare we not imitate him by putting ourselves in subjection to one another?

Jesus practiced the ethic of subordination even when it caused a conflict with self-interest. Jesus' case was like that of two men lost at sea with a one-man boat between them. It raised the question if one should save his life at the loss of another or save another's life at the loss of his own. This was the agonizing conflict of Gethsemane. At the end, Jesus went down that we might be rescued. He could do nothing less than subordinate himself to us in one grand act of self-sacrifice.

At the cross the enemies of Jesus declared a great truth unknowingly when they said he saved others but was unable to save himself. Jesus unquestionably had power to save himself, but it is equally true that he could not exercise that power. One word from Jesus' mouth would have brought legions of angels to paralyze the hands raised against him, but if Jesus had saved himself, he would have been unable to save others. The world would remain lost and hopeless.

Consequences

What are we to make of this? Because Christ subjected himself to all, it is a Christian duty to think of everything not as it affects ourselves only, but also as it affects others. If we refuse Jesus' example of love and subordination, we reject his mission, dishonor his work, and dismiss the model for ministry.

Jesus' model of submission always works better than coercion. To enforce our will, never giving in, always causes hatred and malice. If the church is to have the peace and unity necessary to take the gospel to the whole world, it must learn that a helpful hand is stronger than an arm of power. "If we all pull in one direction," says an old Yiddish proverb, "the world will keel over."

Questions for Discussion

1. What was Hitler's philosophy of rule? Why did he fail?

2. Why are relationships that must be maintained by force doomed?

3. What is the New Testament principle of mutual submission?

4. Explain how Ephesians 5:21-6:9 teaches the ethic of mutual and reciprocal obligation.

5. Explain why our freedom in Christ does not release us from subjection to one another.

6. How may Christians misuse their freedom in Christ?

7. How do we know that brotherly love and freedom must never be separated?

8. Explain how subordination to others is the highest exercise of freedom. What are the implications for any relationship among Christians that forces one to answer to another against his will?

9. What are some of the ways Jesus subjected himself to others?

10. Why does the ethic of mutual submission promote unity among believers?

Number 4

Submit to Others Because You Fear Christ

The Greek New Testament says that we should submit our-selves to one another "in the fear (*phobos*) of Christ" (Ephesians 5:21). Because this is the only passage of the New Testament where the phrase "fear of Christ" occurs, the apostle's appeal seems irregular to some. Conversely, Paul often encourages us to find motivation for ethical action in the love and goodness of God. For example, he urges us, "in view of God's mercy," to become living sacrifices (Romans 12:1), to glorify God for his great mercy (Romans 15:9), and to live a life of love because Christ loved us (Ephesians 5:2), but he never, except in Ephesians 5:21, seeks to motivate us to act "in the fear of Christ."

Because Paul appeals to the "fear of Christ" as motivation for ethical conduct only in Ephesians 5:21, some think that he intended a meaning other than the literal fear that the word *phobos* suggests. They argue that if Paul calls upon us to obey Christ because of fear, he contradicts himself. Elsewhere he said, "For you did not receive a spirit that makes you a slave again to fear, but you received the Spirit of sonship. And by him we cry, 'Abba,' Father"(Romans 8:15).

Because the formula, "in the fear of Christ" seems contra-dictory, and because interpreters recoil from the thought that anything good can come from a relationship with God that finds motivation in fear, translators tend to soften the sharp edge of the Greek by substituting words like "reverence," "awe," or "respect" for the word "fear." I feel, however, that Paul would have used another word if he wanted to exclude the attitude or emotion of fear. The raw word "fear" best corresponds to the Greek word *phobos*.

The apostle's suggestion that we have a literal fear of Christ does, unquestionably, create a problem for those who wish to make the scriptures appeal to the masses. Paul's call for ethical conduct based on the motivation of fear is offensive, not only to many translators, but to the minds of many modern readers as well. People generally relate fear to uncertainty, which robs the mind of its powers of acting and reasoning. Thus nothing good can come of a relationship, either with God or our fellow man, that finds ethical motivation in fear. Even so, we cannot sacrifice the apostle's precise meaning just to make him more palatable to modern readers.

Love and Fear

Another problem with obedience motivated by fear of Christ is a statement made by the apostle John. He taught that love dispels fear and gives us confidence on the Day of Judgment. He said,

> And so we know and rely on the love God has for us. God is love. Whoever lives in love lives in God, and God in him. In this way, love is made complete among us so that we will have confidence on the day of judgment, because in this world we are like him. There is no fear in love. But perfect love drives out fear, because fear has to do with punishment. The one who fears is not made perfect in love (1 John 4:16-18).

John's point is that the person who views God only as a Lawgiver and Judge expects to be punished. The one who knows that God is love expects only acceptance. Thus love displaces fear, leaving assurance in its place.

All this raises an important question. Does John intend to say that because God is love we are to have absolutely no fear of him? Not likely, for John both accepts and conveys the angel's message that we must "Fear God and give him glory" (Revelation 14:7).

No writer of the New Testament understood more fully the nature of God than John. Because he knew God is love, his epistles affirm more clearly the security of believers than any of the other New Testament letters. Yet he feared God, and advises others to fear God as well.

Love is, of course, the most powerful motivation for continued obedience to Christ. Many become Christians because they are afraid to continue in sin. They hear sermons that warn of a terrible God who will destroy the wicked with "everlasting punishment." Moved by dismay and trepidation they become Christians. Yet fear soon gives way to love. As new Christians continue to live in the Lord and his word, they come to see Jesus, not just as a stern judge, but as savior and friend. They learn to love Jesus because he first loved them, and in that love they find the only sufficient motivation for a lifetime of obedience.

Something else must be said. One reason I fear Christ is because of a firsthand experience with his powerful provision and overwhelming love. Thus Paul may be saying in Ephesians 5:21 that we should submit ourselves to one another in "the fear of Christ," not because he is a tyrannical judge, but because he is a friend whose love is interminable and immense. In a similar way the wife submits to her husband in fear (*phobeomia*), not because he is a tyrant, but because he loves her as he loves himself (Ephesians 5:33).

In Genesis 22 we have the story of Abraham offering his son Isaac as a sacrifice. The command to sacrifice Isaac presented Abraham with a set of conflicting moral obligations. Abraham wanted to obey God, but God had never before demanded human sacrifice. Abraham also had to contend with the painful prospect of killing his son—a son of promise born in Abraham's old age—a son he loved more than his life. How could Abraham make a choice between God and Isaac? How could he satisfy such mutually exclusive demands? Genesis 22:12 tells us that Abraham was ready to sacrifice Isaac because he "feared God."

Abraham feared God, not because he felt that God was a terrible tyrant, but because he sensed God's constant compassion. Such fear produces courageous, heroic acts. No matter how much one's soul may tremble, this kind of fear emboldens one to step forward to obey the Lord's most difficult commands.

Jesus also speaks of fear that is motivated by God's goodness. He says,

> I tell you, my friends, do not be afraid of those who kill the body and after that can do no more. But I will show you whom you should fear: Fear him who, after the killing of the body, has power to throw you into hell. Yes, I tell you, fear him. Are not five sparrows sold for two pennies? Yet not one of them is forgotten by God. Indeed, the very hairs of your head are all numbered. Don't be afraid; you are worth more than many sparrows (Luke 12:4-7).

Jesus begins by saying that we should not fear other men because they have power over this life only. Someone may destroy physical life, but it is impossible for him to destroy the soul. Jesus ends by saying that we should fear God alone because he has power to destroy the soul. Yet the immediate appeal is not to a horrible God, but a loving God—a God whose eyes watch over sparrows—a God who watches us closely and loves us immensely.

Characteristic of Paul

The motive of fear in obedience is characteristic of Paul's message. After telling the Corinthians that we must all "stand before the judgment seat of Christ, that each one may receive what is due him for the things done while in the body, whether good or bad," he went on to say, "Since, then, we know what it is to fear the Lord, we try to persuade men" (2 Corinthians 5:10-11). Paul warns against arousing "the Lord's jealousy" in 1 Corinthians 10:22. Also, he uses strong language to describe the judgment of God when he says,

> All this is evidence that God's judgment is right, and as a result you will be counted worthy of the kingdom of God,

for which you are suffering. God is just: He will pay back
trouble to those who trouble you and give relief to you who
are troubled, and to us as well. This will happen when the
Lord Jesus is revealed from heaven in blazing fire with his
powerful angels. He will punish those who do not know God
and do not obey the gospel of our Lord Jesus. They will be
punished with everlasting destruction and shut out from the
presence of the Lord and from the majesty of his power on
the day he comes to be glorified in his holy people and to be
marveled at among all those who have believed. This
includes you, because you believed our testimony to you (2
Thessalonians 1:5-10).

Paul's warning that Christians should subject themselves to
one another "in the fear of Christ" is therefore consistent with
his message to all the churches. If condemnation of the
Christian who refuses to submit to others seems unfair, remember that the attitude that always insists on its own rights can
never be Christ-like, for Christ subordinated himself to all.
Only a carnal mind can remain interested totally in self. Only
pride leads one to demand rigorously from others what he
thinks they owe him. The one who always insists on his rights
shows a lack of humility, love, and concern for others, without
which, he is unfit for the eternal fellowship of God's people.
We must, then, submit ourselves to one another in fear of the
Christ who will punish the disobedient.

Implications for Eternity

In fairness it must be said that Luke 12 is a chapter of alter-
nate encouragement and warning. Although Jesus encourages
us to fear God because of his great love and provision, he ends
with a clear statement of God's terror. Jesus says,

I tell you, whoever acknowledges me before men, the Son of
Man will also acknowledge him before the angels of God.
But he who disowns me before men will be disowned before
the angels of God. And everyone who speaks a word against
the Son of Man will be forgiven, but anyone who blasphemes
against the Holy Spirit will not be forgiven (Luke 12:8-10).

"Fear" (*phobos*) in Ephesians 5:21 is a warning as well. We cannot escape the truth that inherent in the word *phobos* is a warning of eternal punishment to those who refuse to subject themselves to others. To refuse Christ's command that we facilitate the faith, joy, and success of others, when he sacrificed everything for us, is to sin against the love of Christ. The sin of selfishness and insubordination breaks more than a law, it breaks the heart of our Lord. We then come under the condemnation of the unmerciful servant of Matthew 18:19-34:

Again, I tell you that if two of you on earth agree about anything you ask for, it will be done for you by my Father in heaven. For where two or three come together in my name, there am I with them."

Then Peter came to Jesus and asked, "Lord, how many times shall I forgive my brother when he sins against me? Up to seven times?"

Jesus answered, "I tell you, not seven times, but seventy-seven times.

"Therefore, the kingdom of heaven is like a king who wanted to settle accounts with his servants. As he began the settlement, a man who owed him ten thousand talents was brought to him. Since he was not able to pay, the master ordered that he and his wife and his children and all that he had be sold to repay the debt.

"The servant fell on his knees before him. 'Be patient with me,' he begged, 'and I will pay back everything.' The servant's master took pity on him, canceled the debt and let him go.

"But when that servant went out, he found one of his fellow servants who owed him a hundred denarii. He grabbed him and began to choke him. 'Pay back what you owe me!' he demanded.

"His fellow servant fell to his knees and begged him, 'Be patient with me, and I will pay you back.'

"But he refused. Instead, he went off and had the man thrown into prison until he could pay the debt. When the other servants saw what had happened, they were greatly distressed and went and told their master everything that had happened.

"Then the master called the servant in. 'You wicked servant,' he said, 'I canceled all that debt of yours because you begged me to. Shouldn't you have had mercy on your fellow servant just as I had on you?' In anger his master turned him over to the jailers to be tortured, until he should pay back all he owed."

If eternal ruin seems too harsh for the one who refuses to subject himself to others, remember that Christ emptied himself for the sinful world. How can we stand justified before the eternal judge, who sacrificed everything for us, if we refuse the same kindness to others?

We must not forget that Paul said we should submit ourselves to one another "in the fear of Christ." Inherent in the word fear (*phobos*) is the idea of terror, apprehension and horror. The one who refuses to practice the principle of mutual subordination comes under the stinging judgment of God. It is therefore wise for us to subordinate ourselves to others, not for their sake only, but for our own sake as well. Because the aggressive, insubordinate Christian must answer to God for his recalcitrant behavior, stubbornness is ill advised and reckless. How will the selfish, self-serving person stand before a selfless savior?

Questions for Discussion

1. Why does Paul's appeal to the "fear of Christ" in Ephesians 5:21 seem contradictory?

2. Why should one fear a friendly, compassionate God?

3. What does it mean to fear God?

4. If God is not a terrible tyrant, why should we fear him?

5. How do we know that the motive of fear is characteristic of Paul's message? Give examples.

6. Is it fair for God to judge the insubordinate? Why?

7. How does love dispel the fear of God and judgment?

8. Why is love the most powerful motivation for obeying God?

9. Why is it wise to fear God?

10. Why is it in one's self-interest to submit to others?

> "If we make our goal to live a life of compassion
> and unconditional love, then the world will indeed
> become a garden where all kinds of flowers
> can bloom and grow."
> —Elisabeth Kübler-Ross

Number 5
Accept One Another

Homer, in the *Odyssey*, had Odysseus describe a visit to Hades. Among other things, Odysseus saw Sisyphus, king of Corinth, doomed to spend eternity performing a hopeless task. His job was to roll a large boulder from the valley below to the top of a mountain. Sisyphus would strain, tug and sweat to get the job done. Each time, just as he was about to shove the boulder over the crest, it would slip and roll back down the mountain. In spite of disappointment on top of disappointment, Sisyphus would begin the oppressive task all over again.

Accepting others, giving in to them for the common good, can be a tiring, frustrating experience as well. We are often tempted to say, "I've had enough. I quit. I won't let others abuse and bruise me any longer. Its time for someone to give in to me for a change."

We sometimes feel like the battered youngster who played football for a green, immature football team of a small college in the Midwest. As a matter of courtesy, a large university team played the small college each year. Naturally, the large university won every game by a large score. One year the thrashing was especially pitiless. The score was something like seventy to zero at the half. In the third quarter, a lineman for the small school stood up, in the middle of a play, ripped off his helmet, tossed it a full forty yards, and then stormed off the field of play. His coach yelled, "Get back in there, the game isn't over yet." The bruised youngster shouted back, "It's over for me! We came down here to get experience, and I've got it."

It isn't always easy to defer to others, especially when they are weak or lacking in knowledge. It doesn't seem fair that we should be expected always to give in to others for the common good. For a change, we would like for someone to think about what is best for us.

Then, there are those who are constant complainers. They always seem unhappy. They argue with every decision that others make. They always seem to find fault with other's conclusions. They question motives. It seems that they were "born in the objective case and kickative mood."

Because many of us place a high premium on individualism, and because many of us hold strong opinions, we sense the same hopelessness of Sisyphus as we struggle to stand under the New Testament principle of mutual submission. Still, we must keep on trying. If we never give up, with God's help, we will reach the summit.

Beyond the need for persistence, one thing more needs to be said for those who may have trouble obeying the principle of mutual subordination and edification. It is important to remember that *nothing succeeds like courage*. As you work at accepting others whose opinions and lifestyles are different to yours, you will be confronted by fear and failure. Be courageous! Never give up! You will succeed.

A Plain Command

Though it may seem difficult, the scriptures plainly call upon believers everywhere, both those who are narrow in their views, and those who are broad in their application of Christian principles, to submit to one another. Paul says,

> Accept him whose faith is weak, without passing judgment on disputable matters. One man's faith allows him to eat everything, but another man, whose faith is weak, eats only vegetables. The man who eats everything must not look

down on him who does not, and the man who does not eat everything must not condemn the man who does, for God has accepted him. Who are you to judge someone else's servant? To his own master he stands or falls. And he will stand, for the Lord is able to make him stand (Romans 14:1-4).

Not only does the apostle obligate us to subject ourselves to one another, but also he says that we should *accept one another.* Only when we accept one another, with all our varied feelings, conclusions, tastes, temperaments and lifestyles, are we able to practice the rule of mutual subordination. Paul therefore commanded,

Accept one another, then, just as Christ accepted you, in order to bring praise to God. For I tell you that Christ has become a servant of the Jews on behalf of God's truth, to confirm the promises made to the patriarchs so that the Gentiles may glorify God for his mercy, as it is written: "Therefore I will praise you among the Gentiles; I will sing hymns to your name." Again, it says, "Rejoice, O Gentiles, with his people." And again, "Praise the Lord, all you Gentiles, and sing praises to him, all you peoples." And again, Isaiah says, "The Root of Jesse will spring up, one who will arise to rule over the nations; the Gentiles will hope in him" (Romans 15:7-12).

Paul says that we should accept one another as Christ accepted us. Christ accepted us freely, without regard to our differing tastes and temperaments. Jews and Gentiles were so far apart philosophically, religiously and emotionally, that it is difficult to imagine how the two could ever be one in Christ. It spite of their differences, Christ accepted both, and he expected both Jews and Gentiles to accept one another.

In spite of differences, Jews and Gentiles could defer to one another, building up one another. If Christ died for all, and accepted all, they also could accept one another.

Why?

Not only does Paul tell us how to accept one another—*just as Christ accepted you*—but he also tells us why we should accept one another. We should accept one another *in order to bring praise to God.*

God is always glorified when Christians accept one another. Nowhere is this seen more clearly than in Jesus prayer of John 17:20-23:

> My prayer is not for them alone. I pray also for those who will believe in me through their message, *that* all of them may be one, Father, just as you are in me and I am in you. May they also be in us so that the world may believe that you have sent me. I have given them the glory that you gave me, that they may be one as we are one: I in them and you in me. May they be brought to complete unity to let the world know that you sent me and have loved them even as you have loved me."

If for no other reason, we should accept one another for God's sake. Materialism and hedonism characterize this age. Like the Gentile world of the first century, the world today neither glorifies God nor gives him thanks. This present age boasts of its wisdom, but it is foolish. It claims enlightenment, but remains in the dark. The greatest need of this hour is for believers everywhere to accept one another. Our acceptance of one another will prove to the world that God exists, that God sent his son, that God loves us, and that we love one another. Our charming manner of life, like a magnet, will then draw others to Christ. Not only will God be glorified, but his great decision at Calvary will be vindicated as well.

Cooperation and Nature

The problem is that it is easy to know how and why we should accept one another and difficult to find the resolve or the strength of will to do the task. How will we become a group of people who accept others whose opinions, tastes, temperaments and lifestyles are different form our own.

One thing that will help us to accept others is the knowledge that *acceptance of others, and cooperation with them, is natural.* Unity is the God-given goal or destiny, not only of Christians, but also of all mankind.

Thinkers have always talked of unity as a goal of nature. Marcus Aurelius, one of Rome's emperors and highest thinkers, believed that we are made for cooperation, like feet, like hands, like eyelids, like the rows of upper and lower teeth. He believed that for us to act against one another is contrary to nature.

Jawaharlal Nehru, the Cambridge educated Indian statesman, felt that the law of life should not be the competition of acquisitiveness, but cooperation, the good of each contributing to the good of all.

In my travels to the archaeological sites of Egypt, I have marveled at that ancient civilization with its sphinx and pyramids. Words fail me as I try to describe the many Roman architectural treasures that I've seen. The Roman Empire, and every developed nation with it codes and culture, developed because of unified effort. Those who work together toward a common goal attain success. Excessive individualism contributes little to the common good.

If the church is to have a positive effect on a lost world, it also must learn that acceptance of others, and cooperation with them, is its destiny—its God-given nature. Otherwise, the church will remain weak and ineffective. Because of an uncooperative spirit, members of the Corinthian church remained "babes in Christ" (1 Corinthians 3:1). Their suspicions, hatred, jealousies, greed and intolerance, blotted out the possibility of attaining spiritual maturity. Excessive individualism and bias caused them to turn inward. Their introverted lives and antisocial behavior made the Corinthian Christians incapable of reaching out in love to a lost world. They failed because they were unable to put down the spirit of selfishness and competition.

Acceptance and Agreement

For those who find it difficult to accept others, it is also helpful to know that *acceptance does not always mean agreement*. We can see this principle at work in our families. I sometimes say, jokingly, that my wife has never yet agreed that I am perfect. I often disagree with her, and my children, yet my acceptance of them remains unquestioned.

Just here, it is important to remember that Paul could not accept the legalists who preached that men were justified by obedience to the Law of Moses. Also, John refused to accept Gnostics who denied that there was a relationship between the man Jesus, and the Messiah who died on the cross. Some ideas were destructive. When others showed disregard for life or death principles of scripture, the apostles attacked.

Still, it is also important to remember that the apostles chose when to fight. They knew when to fight, and what matters were worthy of a fight. Also, they never fought with others over matters of opinion, unless someone wanted to make of an opinion a law that all others were then obligated to obey.

My impression is that most division and strife among Christians is caused by differing tastes, temperaments, and inconsequential opinions or lifestyles. While our opinions are important to us, they mean nothing to God, and we should find a way to give in to others, and accept them. Frankly, I feel that my opinions are better than those of anyone who disagrees with me. Yet I would never demand that others conform to my views before I accept them Again, in matters of opinion, *acceptance does not always mean agreement.*

For those who feel that they must oppose all differing views because "it is wrong for Christians to compromise their convictions," I can only say that the apostle Paul clearly calls upon us to accept one another, though our opinions may differ. He says,

> One man considers one day more sacred than another; another man considers every day alike. Each one should be fully convinced in his own mind. He who regards one day as special, does so to the Lord. He who eats meat, eats to the Lord, for he gives thanks to God; and he who abstains, does so to the Lord and gives thanks to God. For none of us lives to himself alone and none of us dies to himself alone. If we live, we live to the Lord; and if we die, we die to the Lord. So, whether we live or die, we belong to the Lord. For this very reason, Christ died and returned to life so that he might be the Lord of both the dead and the living. You, then, why do you judge your brother? Or why do you look down on your brother? For we will all stand before God's judgment

seat. It is written: "'As surely as I live,' says the Lord, 'every knee will bow before me; every tongue will confess to God.'" So then, each of us will give an account of himself to God. Therefore let us stop passing judgment on one another. Instead, make up your mind not to put any stumbling block or obstacle in your brother's way" (Romans 14:5-13).

The apostle's command that we stop passing judgment on others and that we accept them, notwithstanding their differing views or opinions, is a difficult task to perform. Still, I want to encourage you to begin. If at the first you fail and feel frustrated, don't give up. In time you will become good at being a shepherd of others. Always remember that the obligation to put others first, like all other duties of Christian living, requires discipline and practice to make perfect. There are no shortcuts to spiritual maturity. Begin today by planting a seed of kindness. Accept others. God will bless you in advance for the fruit that will form from the germ you plant. Meanwhile, the journey will be wonderful, for the joy of travel is not the final destination, but what we see and become along the way.

Questions for Discussion

1. Why do we find the command to accept one another frustrating?

2. What does it mean to accept others as Christ accepted us?

3. How does our acceptance of one another glorify God?

4. What practical advice would you give to someone who has trouble accepting anyone who differs with his opinions?

5. List some illustrations from nature that show how God intended for mankind to cooperate.

6. Do you agree that acceptance of others and agreement with others are different? Can we have one without the other? Explain.

7. How can we accept differing opinions without compromising our convictions?

8. How do we overcome the fear of those who are different from us?

9. How important are our opinions?

10. Read carefully Romans 14. What is the apostle trying to say?

Number 6

Love One Another

I became aware of how willing love is to sacrifice for others when I checked old bank receipts in an effort to discover how I had spent all my money. I made an average salary and lived conservatively, yet had very little savings. Why? Canceled checks told a story of three children with physical and educational needs, of generous love for six grandchildren, and of a widowed mother in financial need. Also, there were church contributions, favorite charities, and special gifts to Christian camps. I learned that love gives everything.

Love constrains us to reach out for the sake of others, even when it causes us pain and suffering. Those who love can put others above themselves, even when doing so demands that they go far beyond what they thought possible.

Because love embraces others, sharing life and warmth, it is impossible for a spirit of competition or disunity to exist between those who have genuine affection for one another. It is not therefore surprising that Paul wrote his magnificent treatise on love to a church fraught with division. Human wisdom would expect the apostle to write the glorious message of 1 Corinthians 13 to some grand church like Antioch, Jerusalem or Philippi. Instead, Paul directed his lofty message of love to a church where he detected an ugly spirit of rivalry and discord.

The Corinthians, for example, fought over preachers. Some pursued Paul. Others followed Apollos or Peter. Some were jealous and quarrelsome (1 Corinthians 3:3), filing lawsuits against other Christians (1 Corinthians 6:1-8). There was division over whether Paul was an apostle, over eating meat offered to idols, spiritual gifts, and the Lord's Supper.

Paul wrote his wonderful exposition on love to the Corinthian Christians because, despite their many spiritual gifts, they lacked the one gift that makes harmony and cooperation possible. Because the Corinthian Christians lacked love, they were hopelessly divided. So Paul purposely targeted Corinth for his great discourse on love.

The Highest Gift

It is important to note that 1 Corinthians 13 follows a chapter in which the apostle talks about Christian unity in the midst of differing gifts. Because Paul detected a certain spiritual competition in the Corinthian flock, he said, in effect, "You Corinthians, despite your many gifts, will never become a successful, joyous church until you become ambitious for the higher gifts." He says,

> Now you are the body of Christ, and each one of you is a part of it. And in the church God has appointed first of all apostles, second prophets, third teachers, then workers of miracles, also those having gifts of healing, those able to help others, those with gifts of administration, and those speaking in different kinds of tongues. Are all apostles? Are all prophets? Are all teachers? Do all work miracles? Do all have gifts of healing? Do all speak in tongues? Do all interpret? But eagerly desire the greater gifts. And now I will show you the most excellent way. If I speak in the tongues of men and of angels, but have not love, I am only a resounding gong or a clanging cymbal. If I have the gift of prophecy and can fathom all mysteries and all knowledge, and if I have a faith that can move mountains, but have not love, I am nothing. If I give all I possess to the poor and surrender my body to the flames, but have not love, I gain nothing (1 Corinthians 12:27-13:3).

Love is the highest gift because it alone supplies the motivation that makes it possible for other gifts to take shape and find expression. Someone, for example, may have the kind of courage that would sacrifice everything for the poor, but unless there is love for the poor, that courage will likely remain dormant. Someone may be perfectly able to attain such heights of selflessness and goodwill for others that he finds it a joy to practice the principle of subjection to others, but without love it is improbable that he will ever take responsibility for the fulfillment of another. Consequently the New Testament repeatedly calls upon us to love one another. The following passages show the importance of loving others:

> A new command I give you: *Love one another*. As I have loved you, so you *must love one another* (John 13:34).
>
> By this all men will know that you are my disciples, if you *love one another* (John 13:35).
>
> Let no debt remain outstanding, except the continuing debt to *love one another*, for he who loves his fellowman has fulfilled the law (Romans 13:8).
>
> Now that you have purified yourselves by obeying the truth so that you have sincere love for your brothers, *love one another* deeply, from the heart (1 Peter 1:22).
>
> This is the message you heard from the beginning: We should *love one another* (1 John 3:11).
>
> And this is his command: to believe in the name of his Son, Jesus Christ, and to *love one another* as he commanded us (1 John 3:23).
>
> Dear friends, let us *love one another*, for love comes from God. Everyone who loves has been born of God and knows God (1 John 4:7).
>
> Dear friends, since God so loved us, we also ought to *love one another* (1 John 4:11).
>
> No one has ever seen God; but if we *love one another*, God lives in us and his love is made complete in us (1 John 4:12).
>
> And now, dear lady, I am not writing you a new command but one we have had from the beginning. I ask that we *love one another* (2 John 1:5).

Besides the above passages from the New International Version, two additional verses occur in the Authorized Version. Jesus says, "These things I command you, that you *love one another*" (John 15:17). Paul says, "But as touching brotherly love ye need not that I write unto you: for ye yourselves are taught of God to *love one another*" (1 Thessalonians 4:9).

Repetition and Importance

What are we to make of this? When an idea occurs repeatedly in the scriptures, it deserves special attention. A statement repeated often is God's way of saying, "This is more important than the rest." Because the command to "love one another" occurs so often in scripture, it ranks highest in God's train of commands.

Many feel uncomfortable with the idea that some Bible passages are more important than others are. I recall hearing a sermon several years ago in which the preacher said that John 14 was his favorite chapter of the New Testament. Then, for fear that he had left his congregation with the impression that other passages were less important, he hurriedly concluded, "I should not have said that John 14 is my favorite New Testament chapter since all scriptures are equally important, and we shouldn't have favorites."

Paul would not agree. He said to the Corinthians that the resurrection was a matter of "first importance" (1 Corinthians 15:3). While the apostle felt that every passage he wrote provided illumination for the Christian way, everything paled in the glorious light of the resurrection.

Jesus also felt that some things are more important than others are. When asked what was the most important command, Jesus answered, "Love the Lord your God with all your heart and with all your soul and with all your mind and with all your strength. The second is this: Love your neighbor as yourself. There is no commandment greater than these" (Mark 12:30-31).

All this raises an important question. How do we decide which scriptures are more important than others are? May we make an arbitrary choice or is there a formula by which we arrive at the most important ideas of God's word? One way to decide which scriptures are most important is to look at how often they occur. A passage repeated is very important. Another way to know that a passage is more important than the rest is by its claims. We know, for example, that the resurrection is the most important event in Paul's letters because he makes a claim for its priority (1 Corinthians 15:3).

The command to love one another not only occurs often in the scripture, but Jesus said plainly that the only obligation greater than love for others is the obligation to love God (Mark 12:30-31). An inescapable truth emerges. Because nothing takes precedence over love, the believer who cannot first love others may as well forget the rest. Without love, it is impossible to be a Christian.

Love Empowers

Paul argues in Romans that love empowers us to keep all the other commands of God. He also states that only love makes it possible for us to do no harm to others. He says,

> Let no debt remain outstanding, except the continuing debt to love one another, for he who loves his fellowman has fulfilled the law. The commandments, "Do not commit adultery," "Do not murder," "Do not steal," "Do not covet," and whatever other commandment there may be, are summed up in this one rule: "Love your neighbor as yourself." Love does no harm to its neighbor. Therefore love is the fulfillment of the law (Romans 13:8-10).

For the one who loves, everything is clear—how to act, where to go, how to think, what to do—it all takes care of itself. Love never asks anybody anything because it never doubts its motive. Love prefers to serve. Its only motive is to advance others. The person who loves is happy when others receive promotion and he is overlooked. Because envy cannot live in a heart filled with love, a lover takes pleasure when others receive honor. Love always seeks the other person's highest good.

Since Jesus always sought the highest good of others, it isn't surprising to discover that he chose us for a life of love as well. He said,

> I have told you this so that my joy may be in you and that your joy may be complete. My command is this: Love each other as I have loved you. Greater love has no one than this, that he lay down his life for his friends. You are my friends if you do what I command. I no longer call you servants, because a servant does not know his master's business. Instead, I have called you friends, for everything that I learned from my Father I have made known to you. You did not choose me, but I chose you and appointed you to go and bear fruit—fruit that will last. Then the Father will give you whatever you ask in my name. This is my command: Love each other (John 15:11-17).

Love and Spirituality

The message is clear. Genuine love for others is the mark of a spiritual person. Christians vary in their views about what makes a person spiritual. Some feel that the highly vocal person who continually talks religion is spiritual. Others think that the one who prays frequently deserves the reputation of being more spiritual than the rest. While it is true that tumultuous praise and regular prayers may be compatible with spirituality, they in no way constitute spirituality or prove its presence.

The one mark of true spirituality is love. The spiritual person knows that it is not his purpose to compete with others or dispute and quarrel with others, but to love others as Christ loved us. Many people claim spirituality whose lives are a demonstration of selfishness. They think only of themselves. They cannot be helpers and partners to others. Only the person who loves can ever be genuine enough to serve others as Christ served us at Calvary.

Because love is, above all, the gift of oneself, it always finds a way, no matter the cost, to subordinate itself to others. Subordination to others may call upon one to go far beyond what he ever imagined—to make a greater sacrifice than he thought possible. Yet love casts out the fear of going the extra mile, and finds a way to sacrifice all for others (1 John 4:18).

Solomon said, "Many waters cannot quench love; rivers cannot wash it away" (Song of Songs 8:7). Because love never fails, it is always the mark that identifies a stable, mature faith. Without spiritual maturity we will never attain the joy and unity God intended for his people. Let us therefore love one another, as Christ loved us.

Questions for Discussion

1. What is love?

2. Why does love stir us to go the extra mile in our relationships with others?

3. How does love give all to others without questioning or even being aware of the sacrifice? Think of examples in your life when, because of your love, you gave all without questioning.

4. Why did Paul write his great message of love to the Corinthian church?

5. Why is love the highest gift?

6. Why do the scriptures repeat the command to love one another so often?

7. How may we know that some ideas of God's word are more important than others are? May we make an arbitrary choice or is there a formula that will help us find the most important ideas of the scriptures?

8. Why is it impossible to be a Christian without love?

9. Why is love the mark of spirituality?

10. Why is love the fulfillment of the law (Romans 13:8-10)?

> "We have committed the Golden Rule to memory;
> let us now commit it to life."
> —Edwin Markham

Number 7

Live in Harmony
with One Another

Somewhere I heard the story of a General and his young aide, a Lieutenant, who traveled from base to base on military business following World War II in Europe. They usually traveled by train. One of their trips found them in a compartment with two women—a grandmother, and her beautiful granddaughter.

Time passed rapidly and pleasantly, as it always does when you are in good company. Suddenly, the train broke into the total darkness of a long, black tunnel. No one was able to see anything, but everyone was impressed with two distinct sounds—the smack of a kiss, and the slap of a face.

When the train broke out into the light at the end of the tunnel, all but one had mixed emotions. It pleased the beautiful young granddaughter that the Lieutenant was so smitten that he stole a kiss from her, but she was displeased that her grandmother slapped him for it. The Grandmother was aghast that the young soldier took advantage of the dark to kiss her granddaughter, but she was glad that her granddaughter slapped him for it. The General found a new respect for an enterprising aide that seized the opportunity and kissed a pretty girl, but he was upset that he got slapped for it. The young Lieutenant was the only one whose emotions were unmixed. His only emotion was unalloyed joy, for he had done two things simultaneously that he always wanted to do—steal a kiss from a pretty girl, and slap his General.

I like this story because, in a humorous way, it speaks to the need for taking advantage of our opportunities when they present themselves. Procrastination often means that we lose our opportunities forever.

The next few pages give me an opportunity to say something I feel is important. I must not lose this occasion to speak from my heart. If I seem too passionate, or a bit bold, I can only say that I write more from deep conviction than agitation.

This church age does not take seriously Paul's command to "Live in harmony with one another" (Romans 12:16). While there is much talk about the need for harmony among believers, strife continues its ugly work. Obviously, many feel that accord is a desirable, but unnecessary spiritual luxury. Yet, the opposite is true. Christianity now exists in the hostile environment of atheism, materialism, hedonism, and a host of other antagonistic forces that will paralyze and destroy the world if the church does not find a way to lay aside the polemics of the past, and rediscover the oneness that enriched the primitive church. Because the church now exists in a setting that makes peace an urgent matter of survival, harmony among Christians must be made to top the list of high priorities.

It will no longer do to dismiss pleas for peace with the words, "We are not ready yet," or "The time is not yet ripe." We have said, "Not yet," for too long. We must make something with, and shape something from, the little time left to us. We cannot afford to remain happy with the *status quo*. Sheer passivity is unacceptable. We can no longer content ourselves with the thought that Christian concord is a nice, but antiquated or archaic idea worthy only of indifference by modern believers. Because contention among Christians constitutes an ongoing disgrace that renders the gospel message both ludicrous and laughable, it is imperative that we attain oneness in Christ.

Jesus' Prayer for Oneness

The foundation upon which the New Testament theme of Christian harmony stands is the prayer of Jesus in John 17:20-23:

My prayer is not for them alone. I pray also for those who
will believe in me through their message, that all of them
may be one, Father, just as you are in me and I am in you.
May they also be in us so that the world may believe that you
have sent me. I have given them the glory that you gave me,
that they may be one as we are one: I in them and you in me.
May they be brought to complete unity to let the world
know that you sent me and have loved them even as you have
loved me.

Owing to Jesus' emphasis on oneness, Paul felt obligated to
remind the Roman Christians that although they were many
members, they formed but one body, and should therefore
strive to be of one mind (Romans 12:4-5, 16). The apostle uses
the same picture in his letter to the Corinthians as he pleads
with them to cease their arguing so that they might be joined
in the same mind (1 Corinthians 12:12-31). He tells the quarreling Corinthians that their differences with one another cause
the kind of discord that reflects a carnal way of thinking that
opposes the mind of Christ (1 Corinthians 3:3). The apostle
urges the Corinthians to live in peace (2 Corinthians 13:11).

To the Ephesians Paul wrote that Jew and Greek are united
as one (Ephesians 2:13-14). Because God demolished the walls
that divide, the Ephesians must maintain peace, remembering
that there is one Lord, one faith, one baptism, and one God
(Ephesians 4:3-6).

Paul's instruction to the Philippians is that they must stand
fast in one spirit, striving together for the faith of the gospel
(Philippians 1:27). They are to be like-minded, having the
same love, spirit and purpose (Philippians 2:2). Two quarreling
women in the Philippian church, Euodia and Syntyche, are to
"agree with each other in the Lord" (Philippians 4:2).

Clearly, the New Testament principle of harmony in Christ is
much more than a very worthwhile, but unnecessary spiritual
luxury. Because religious strife reflects a carnal or fleshly attitude, it calls into question both the gospel and the church.
Christian concord is therefore indispensable to the true nature
of the church. No believer can live a sincere Christian life unless
peace characterizes his relationships with other Christians. The

church can never be Christian in a climate of quarreling and disharmony. The New Testament images of the church as the bride of Christ, the body of Christ, and God's instrument of reconciliation, make it obvious that God's people must live in peace and harmony with one another if they are to form the true church of Christ in the world.

Oneness prevailed among early Christians. Their perpetual awareness of the need to maintain peace formed an innate component of the church. It isn't surprising, then, to read that the primitive church was a sharing group of believers who were of one heart and soul (Acts 4:32). Because they were all baptized into one body, they were all one in Christ Jesus (1 Corinthians 12:8; Galatians 3:28).

Harmony in Diversity

The like-mindedness we strive for can never be the dismal uniformity of bureaucracy. The like-mindedness of the church forms its synthesis from the fabric of diversity. Because we are loyal to the Christ who prayed for us to be one, we strive to preserve peace despite antipathies of position and social standing, race and color, opinions and feelings, and tastes and temperaments.

Consider the diversity of the primitive church. The earliest Christians were Jews who found continuity with the Old Testament. In their view, Jesus came not to abolish, but to fulfill the law and the prophets. The Jerusalem church felt that Christ brought something new, but not something "spanking new." Unlike the Gentile churches mentioned in the latter part of Acts, the church at Jerusalem did not acknowledge a fundamental split between their new status in Christ and their previous life. The Christians at Jerusalem continued to observe the ordinances of Moses, especially circumcision, dietary regulations, and Jewish religious festivals.

Also, there was diversity within the ranks of the Jerusalem church. A minority group, influenced by Greek culture, identified more with the Jewish thought of the Hellenistic Diaspora (Jews influenced by ancient Greece, it's culture and language).

Because the Jerusalem Christians attained peace in this diversity of thought, taste and temperament, they found a means to care for widows of the minority group when "Grecian Jews" complained to the "Hebraic Jews" about the neglect of their widows in the daily distribution of food (Acts 6:1-6).

When converts to Christianity began coming more from pagan than Jewish ranks, the distinction between tastes, temperaments and feelings became more acute. While Jews retained a respect for the ordinances of Moses, Gentiles found them offensive. It doesn't take much imagination to see how ripe the situation was for discord. One group, Hebraic Jews, felt that Christianity should maintain continuity with Judaism, while another group, Hellenistic Jews and Gentiles, felt that Christianity was an entirely new system, with no real ties to the past. The question of continuity between the old and new remained a thorny question for the primitive church, as Paul shows in Galatians. Yet, early on at Jerusalem, it seems that solidarity with Gentile churches prevailed because believers managed to find harmony in their diversity.

There were times, of course, when diversity became intolerable. Consider, for example, the epistle of 1 John. Although John places great emphasis on brotherly love, he is stinging in his condemnation of those who held Gnostic tendencies. They erroneously taught that Christ had no connection with the human Jesus—that he did not come in the flesh (1 John 3:22). This difference went far beyond the dissimilarity of taste, temperament, race and opinion, that existed between Jews and Gentiles. The Gnostics preached a doctrine that denied the incarnation. If Christ did not come in the flesh, then he did not die in the flesh, and there was no resurrection of the flesh. Christianity therefore lacked a foundation of credibility, and the world remained forever without hope.

While it is unquestionably true that the first century church sometimes found diverse opinions unacceptable, what worries me now is a feeling that the modern church tends to be far less permissive of diversity in matters of opinion than the primitive church. I worry that we are less likely to make the give-and-take adjustments that make for peace and harmony.

God and the Barriers that Divide

When we are intolerant of differing lifestyles, tastes, temperaments and opinions, we are unlike God. According to Paul, God opens the way to oneness by removing all barriers that promote human separation. The apostle says,

> Therefore, remember that formerly you who are Gentiles by birth and called "uncircumcised" by those who call themselves "the circumcision" (that done in the body by the hands of men)—remember that at that time you were separate from Christ, excluded from citizenship in Israel and foreigners to the covenants of the promise, without hope and without God in the world. But now in Christ Jesus you who once were far away have been brought near through the blood of Christ. For he himself is our peace, who has made the two one and has destroyed the barrier, the dividing wall of hostility, by abolishing in his flesh the law with its commandments and regulations. His purpose was to create in himself one new man out of the two, thus making peace, and in this one body to reconcile both of them to God through the cross, by which he put to death their hostility. He came and preached peace to you who were far away and peace to those who were near. For through him we both have access to the Father by one Spirit (Ephesians 2:11-18).

Because Moses' law was a wall that divided Jew and Gentile, God abolished it by Christ's death on the cross. With the abolition of the Law, God broke down the barriers that divided mankind. What were the barriers? The name "Gentiles" suggested that some were in humanity's wrong half. The infamous descriptive phrase, "called uncircumcised," conveyed the message that the Gentiles did not carry in their flesh the required mark of the one true faith. "Separate from Christ" marked the Gentiles as those who lived without knowledge or communion with God's only son. "Excluded from citizenship in Israel" meant that the Gentiles lacked fellowship with God's chosen people. "Foreigners to the covenants of promise" meant that Gentiles lived outside the protection of God's providence. "Without hope," and "without God in the world," the Gentiles lacked brotherhood with the saved people of God.

How can men traverse such separating walls? With men it is impossible. God therefore removed the barriers in Christ. In one grand sacrificial act, Jesus made it possible for mankind—Jew and Gentile—to become one.

It is difficult to imagine two groups more diverse in lifestyle and thought than the Jewish and Gentile Christians of the first-century church. Without the cross of Christ, it would be impossible to reconcile their differing views on the ordinances of Moses' law, the kingdom of God, and Christ's Second Coming.

Conclusion

What are we to make of this? If God crushes the evils that seduce and divide men, we also must make every effort to promote harmony among God's people. The task is not easy because, unlike the Jerusalem church, we are not persecuted. Our status is one of pride and sophistication, and we can meet with more than a single congregation or church family. Also, we struggle to cross over barriers that we inherited from prior generations—barriers hallowed by time and tradition. Still, we may not excuse ourselves because our present status is more complicated than that of the Jerusalem church of the first-century. There is no justification for the extremes to which we carry our sectarian views.

The viewpoint of the entire New Testament is that all men are one in Christ. Because all Christians form "one body," they are to pray for one another, serve one another, admonish one another, honor one another, greet one another, forgive one another, be hospitable to one another, and be kind to one another.

Admittedly, the quest for peace and harmony is not easy. I feel, however, that the church can exhibit a genuine oneness before the world if it comes to understand that discord is not proof of deeper knowledge, or of greater willingness to stand for truth, but of sin. We must cease leaving an impression with the world that Christianity consists of nothing more than a series of questions under debate.

Questions for Discussion

1. Explain why Christian harmony is more than a desirable, but unnecessary spiritual luxury.

2. Why is Jesus' prayer of John 17 the foundation upon which the New Testament theme of oneness stands?

3. Explain Paul's analogy of the church to the human body.

4. Why can the church never be Christian in a climate of quarreling and discord?

5. What is the meaning of the New Testament picture of the church as the bride of Christ, body of Christ, and God's reconciling instrument? What do such pictures of the church imply about Christian peace and harmony?

6. Explain the principle of oneness in diversity.

7. In what ways was the New Testament church diverse?

8. When is the principle of unity in diversity unacceptable? Give examples from the New Testament. What are your impressions? Did the New Testament church find diversity unacceptable often? Seldom?

9. What applications can the modern church make of Paul's teaching in Ephesians 2:11-18?

10. How may we promote harmony among Christians? Churches?

> "Did universal charity prevail,
> earth would be a heaven,
> and heaven a fable."
> —Charles Caleb Colton

Number 8

Agree with One Another

Thomas Jefferson felt that human nature is inherently argumentative. In a letter to John Taylor, he argued that "an association of men who will not quarrel with one another is a thing that never yet existed, from the greatest confederacy of nations down to a town meeting or vestry."

In other words, because people are inherently contentious, they instinctively fight their political, philosophical, and religious battles. Because of man's genetic properties, he has a propensity or predilection for conflict that he cannot keep from surfacing.

A superficial observation of human nature does leave the impression that mankind was born to fight. It seems that if humans have nothing more important to fight over they will fight over opinions, words, or they will fight merely because they dislike someone's personality or appearance. It sometimes seems that the human family can never have peace because of a genetic preference for conflict.

The problem I have with the idea that genes decide moral conduct is that it contradicts a cherished Christian anthropology that says human actions are the product of human reason, deliberation, and choice. The explanation of human behavior is not found in mechanical laws of nature, but in free actions determined by rational laws of the mind. I, too, for example, have a strong tendency to be disagreeable and argumentative. I guess it's the Irish in me. But I have learned how to refrain from being contentious, and how to agree with others for the common good. I am agreeable, not because it comes naturally, but because I have decided to do what is best.

Men are argumentative, not because of fate, but because they choose to be self-assertive, believing that there is always a place for a person of force. You must conquer and rule or serve and lose. You hold your unquestionable rights and opinions in the world, not by standing guard, but by attacking—by being the hammer, not the anvil.

What worries me just now is the feeling that Christians often accept the view that self-assertion is a great virtue. I know Christian leaders who feel that churches cannot be built without the exercise of force or power. They feel, as Charles De Gaulle put it in a 1968 *New York Times Magazine* interview, "The perfection preached in the gospels never yet built an empire. Every man of action has a strong dose of egotism, pride, hardness, and cunning." While the oppressive church leaders I know would never be so bold or blunt as De Gaulle, their actions betray a commitment to force for getting desired results.

With self-assertive elders, preachers, deacons, and people in the pews, the churches often find themselves in a struggle to survive. Many churches know firsthand that the most destructive conflicts are wars of opinion fought by unyielding people insisting on their rights. From sad experience they know that when believers use might to exercise right, and make argument their artillery, discord becomes a poisonous parasite gnawing at the bowels of Christian unity.

A Time to Fight

There is a time, of course, for Christians to wage warfare. It is better to fight over a true doctrinal question without settling it than to settle the question without a fight. It is futile for sheep to make rules favoring vegetarianism while wolves remain carnivorous. Nothing will ever make it possible for sheep to lie down with wolves, unless the sheep are inside the wolves. Because Jesus warned of wolves that come in sheep's clothing, we must be watchful, ready to fight fiercely with any enemy who would destroy God's flock.

Jesus confronted the self-righteous religious establishment of his time because it hindered those who sought to enter the kingdom of God. People stumbled under the heavy theological burdens placed upon them by the Scribes and Pharisees—burdens that the Scribes and Pharisees felt no personal obligation to bear. Because hypocritical religious leaders always cause the weak to stumble, it is not surprising that Jesus fought with the religious aristocracy of his time. Jesus' love for honest God-seekers would not allow him to stand quietly by while a self-serving enemy devoured God's people.

Paul fought fiercely with legalistic Jews for the same reason. Although the apostle recognized that the Gentile churches owed their spiritual heritage to the Jews, he could not allow them to divert the attention of Gentiles away from the cross.

Paul fought a heroic battle for a universal, non-legalistic form of Christianity. For the apostle, there was a distinct process of salvation. Men are in sin (Romans 5:12-19). Sinners receive baptism into Christ and begin a new life (Romans 6:1-4). By adoption believers become children of God and partakers of the blessings of Christ (Romans 8:15-17).

Because the blessings of Christ and the resurrection are inseparable, Paul gloried only in the cross (Galatians 6:14). When Jewish teachers persuaded Gentiles to focus attention away from the cross, they became enslaved again to sin. Paul therefore says,

> Formerly, when you did not know God, you were slaves to those who by nature are not gods. But now that you know God—or rather are known by God—how is it that you are turning back to those weak and miserable principles? Do you wish to be enslaved by them all over again? You are observing special days and months and seasons and years! I fear for you, that somehow I have wasted my efforts on you. I plead with you, brothers, become like me, for I became like you. You have done me no wrong (Galatians 4:8-12).

It isn't difficult to see why Paul fought an unrelenting battle with the legalists. The salvation of souls was at risk. Paul's pastoral concern for God's people compelled him to fight the hungry wolves whose heresy would devour God's flock.

The Problem

While it is true that we must defend against the dangers of false teachers, the thing that worries me is that we often cry, "Wolf!" when there is no threat. We fight about things that are unsuitable for fighting. We make loud noises in support of quiet things, and strike each other over gentle things. This church age is overfond of conflict for conflict's sake. Wishing to impose our opinions and rights, we not only make peace and unity impossible, but we also leave a fatal impression with the world that Christianity consists of nothing more than a succession of conflicting ideologies under dispute.

Quarreling among Christians not only makes Christianity undesirable to the world, but it also provides an opening for Satan to discredit the idea of God's existence. If Christians live in a continuous state of strife, how will the world accept the credibility of our claim that Jesus Christ is the Son of God? Because arguments among friends are opportunities for foes, Jesus prayed the following poignant prayer for all his followers:

> My prayer is not for them alone. I pray also for those who will believe in me through their message, that all of them may be one, Father, just as you are in me and I am in you. May they also be in us so that the world may believe that you have sent me. I have given them the glory that you gave me, that they may be one as we are one: I in them and you in me. May they be brought to complete unity to let the world know that you sent me and have loved them even as you have loved me (John 17:20-23).

The Jerusalem Example

Because the world's acceptance of Jesus Christ as God's son depends on Christian agreement, the leadership of the

Jerusalem church sought solidarity with the Gentile churches, though their differences seemed impossible to reconcile.

The persecution that inspired Stephen's martyrdom scattered Christians beyond the borders of Palestine. Missionaries, mostly unknown, took the gospel message to fellow Jews, but in the Syrian capital of Antioch, Greeks heard the faith preached, and Antioch became the center of Christian activity. The disciples were first called "Christians" at Antioch. Inevitably, the question about the relation of Gentile believers to the Jewish Law arose.

While there were many similarities between the Jewish and Gentile churches, there were some profound differences. For one thing, they viewed the kingdom of God differently. It is difficult to imagine that the Jerusalem Christians thought of the church as a permanent society. It was just a temporary arrangement destined to vanish when the kingdom of God appeared. Gentile Christians, though, thought of the church as itself a part of the kingdom—the perfect and finished body of Christ. It logically follows that the relationship between Christ and the Jewish church was different from the relationship between Christ and the Gentile church. The Jewish church looked forward in anticipation of Jesus' immediate return. Among Gentiles churches Jesus was already present and active spiritually.

Also, the Jewish and Gentile churches had profound cultural differences. The Gentile converts came out of paganism. They lacked knowledge of Moses' Law. The Jews had been pious devotees of Moses' legal system for generations. The cultural setting of the church would necessarily have assumed a different form in the Gentile world where most converts were pagan, from that in Jerusalem where converts did not totally cease being Jews merely because they became Christians.

Although there seemed to be irreconcilable differences, the two groups attained solidarity because, as we see in Acts 15, the Jerusalem leadership subjected its opinions and preferences to the Gentile churches. The primary purpose of the Jerusalem council in Acts 15 was to question the role of Jewish laws and customs for Gentiles in the new religion. The rite of circumcision was the chief question of the meeting. Peter argued that

Gentiles should not have the yoke of Jewish law upon their necks (Acts 15:10). Barnabas and Paul said that the rite of circumcision should be dropped for Gentiles, and James concluded that Jews should not require non-Jewish Christians to keep Jewish rites and ceremonies. Thus the Jerusalem church, through a grand act of invincible goodwill, preserved unity and made it possible for Christianity to become not just another Jewish sect, but a universal religion as God intended.

Acquiesce To One Another

Like the leadership of the Jerusalem church, we should seek solidarity with Christians whose lifestyles and opinions are different from ours. The Jerusalem case was extreme. The Gentiles' disregard for Jewish rites and customs clearly posed a threat to the Jewish way of life. Yet the Jewish leaders overcame their fear, and accepted the Gentiles as brothers.

The Jerusalem church, at least in the beginning, conquered the tendency to fight by putting itself in a dialogical relationship with the Gentiles. The Jewish Christians talked with the Gentiles, and through empathy and appreciation for their situation, the Jews became free enough about themselves to see the Gentile's point of view.

Unquestionably, there are times when we must fight. If we must fight, then let us contend fiercely, but let us first make sure that we are fighting over life or death principles, and not just because we want to force our inconsequential opinions or lifestyles on others.

Let us choose to "agree with one another" (1 Corinthians 1:10).

Questions for Discussion

1. What is wrong with the idea that genes determine moral conduct? Why are men argumentative?

2. Why is the self-assertive person divisive?

3. When is it permissible for Christians to differ?

4. Why did Jesus contend with the Scribes and Pharisees?

5. Why did Paul contend with Jewish legalists?

6. Explain how Christian unity gives credibility to the claim that Jesus Christ is God's son.

7. Why does quarreling among Christians make Christianity undesirable?

8. What are some similarities between the Gentile and Jewish churches in the New Testament? Differences?

9. How were the Gentile and Jewish churches able to attain solidarity?

10. How do you distinguish what is a matter of principle from a matter of opinion? Why is a matter of opinion inconsequential?

Number 9

Serve One Another

The meeting began on Sunday morning, and was to continue through the following Sunday night. It was an effort to reach the lost of a remote rural community with the saving message of Christ. Hopefully, the local church would also find a revival of Christian commitment and spirituality.

On Tuesday night, a man came forward during the singing of the invitation hymn, and requested baptism. One of the old men, an elder of the congregation, also approached to inform me that the church had no baptistery, and that he didn't know of a suitable creek or river near enough to immerse the new convert that night. I was upset. I requested that the men of the church make some provision for the baptism at once. They remembered that on one of the nearby farms was a pond for watering livestock, and that it was deep enough for a baptism.

I will never forget the spectacle of a long procession of cars going down a dusty farm road toward that pond. The procession stopped several times as someone ran before the lead car to open what were called "gaps" in the fences. Upon arrival at the livestock pond, a number of cars parked around the banks, shining their headlights into the water.

I took the hand of the one to be baptized and led him out into the water. It was disgusting! We sank into the muddy bottom up to our ankles. A large frog jumped from the bank into the pond with such a loud splash that we both nearly dislodged ourselves from the muddy bottom to walk on the water. We both imagined that the place was home to several poisonous snakes. We entered the water with much fear and consternation.

As I prepared to immerse the man, I asked, "Do you believe that Jesus Christ is the Son of God?" I had asked the same question before at hundreds of baptisms. Like all the others, I expected him to answer, "Yes!" I would then immerse him "in the name of the Father, and the Son, and the Holy Spirit, for the remission of sins" (Mark 16:15-16; Acts 2:38). The problem is that I did not get the answer I anticipated. When I asked, "Do you believe that Jesus Christ is the Son of God?" he looked around at our frightful surroundings and replied, "Young man, what the hell do you think I'm doing in this water?"

Upon hearing his reply, somebody on the bank shouted, "Hey, preacher, dunk him twice!" I didn't. But I am happy to announce that he became a very good Christian.

It occurs to me that baptism is not a magic formula by which one's personality is miraculously transformed. After baptism, one still has to contend with old temptations. When we are born anew in Christ, we are but babes. We reach maturity in Christ only after a lifetime of growth (2 Peter 3:18).

Because the new Christian must have time to overcome old ways, it is natural for him to feel uncomfortable with serving others. The way of the world is to take care of self. Worldly wisdom says, "Never put your neck out for anybody." Consequently, new Christians often find it difficult to serve others at first. But in time, they learn how to put others first.

Consider Paul

Of all the apostles, Paul might have found it easy to think that he could be a Christian without concern for the disciplines and duties of local church life. Unlike Peter and the others, Paul was not present at the beginning of the church in Jerusalem. Unlike the others, Paul did not have the experience of being with Jesus during the years of his personal ministry. Owing to his lack of personal involvement with the inner circle during the years of Jesus' physical presence—a time that taught the early disciples the importance of mutual care and concern for one another—Paul might have found the lifestyle of the Christian individualist acceptable. Yet the opposite is true. Paul was a quick study. He soon became, in the deepest sense, a shepherd of God's flock.

While Paul felt that it was the special obligation of an apostle to serve the church, he also thought that every Christian should attend to the needs of others. He said to the Galatians, "You, my brothers, were called to be free, But do not use your freedom to indulge the sinful nature; rather, *serve one another in love*" (Galatians 5:13).

Paul lacks sympathy for the freelance Christian who says, "Give me Christ but not the church." For Paul, the church was not only a deliberate intention of God, but also a spiritual necessity (Ephesians 5:25-27).

In Paul's thought there was no way of separating Christ and the church. Christ did not leave changed individuals only, but a community. To think of Christ means that one must necessarily think of the church, for the church is Christ's family on earth.

Paul's view of the church as family comes through in his affectionate letter to the Philippians where he says,

I thank my God every time I remember you. In all my prayers for all of you, I always pray with joy because of your partnership in the gospel from the first day until now, being confident of this, that he who began a good work in you will carry it on to completion until the day of Christ Jesus. It is right for me to feel this way about all of you, since I have you in my heart; for whether I am in chains or defending and confirming the gospel, all of you share in God's grace with me. God can testify how I long for all of you with the affection of Christ Jesus. And this is my prayer: that your love may abound more and more in knowledge and depth of insight, so that you may be able to discern what is best and may be pure and blameless until the day of Christ, filled with the fruit of righteousness that comes through Jesus Christ—to the glory and praise of God (Philippians 1:3-11).

Obviously, Paul needed, as we all do, the fellowship of Christians. Because we need one another, the God who places men in families also places solitary Christians in churches for their spiritual health and wellbeing. The church is far more than a local congregation housed in a specific building. It is much more than just a place for Christians to go on Sunday mornings. The church is a place for believers to encourage one another—a place of love and provision in times of trouble, tragedy or disappointment. A "church invisible" is not a family at all. The church fulfills its purpose as the "body of Christ" only when it becomes the concrete embodiment of a family of believers.

The Church as Community

For Paul, Christian faith and life were community, not just the beliefs or lifestyles of scattered individuals. The apostle's famous phrase, "in Christ," always conveys the idea of being "in the church." To take Christ seriously is to take the church seriously. Paul would view the "Christian individualist" as a contradiction.

Paul's view of the church as community meant much more than we usually mean when we talk of fellowship among believers. "Fellowship" is a much-abused word among modern Christians. For many of us, fellowship means friends, food, and fun. For the early church, fellowship was togetherness, sharing, participation, and above all, mutual concern for one another. The wealthy shared with the poor, and the poor blessed the rich with love and humility. If a poor Christian died, other Christians paid for the funeral. They wept genuine tears and displayed sincere feelings of grief at the loss of a family member. No barriers of race, nationality, color or class existed in the church. All men formed one family "in Christ Jesus." As one family, they met from "house to house." No one was excluded. Everyone was included. They shared with each other because each was a part of the other. They drew life from one another.

Paul knew from the beginning of his Christian life that the organized church on earth is the living family of Christ. At the outset of his conversion, while on the Damascus road, he discovered that the one who touches the church touches Christ as well. "Saul, Saul," the Lord asked, "Why do you persecute me?" We have no knowledge that Paul ever saw Jesus until this moment. Even if Paul had seen Jesus during his life on earth, the Lord now sits at God's right hand, far out of range of any personal harm Paul might seek to inflict. Why, then, does Jesus take Paul's persecution of Christians as a personal affront? Clearly, Jesus felt the very pain of his persecuted people. Here, at the outset of his Christian life, Paul discovered a truth that controlled his thinking about the church for the rest of his life. For Paul, the church was always the incarnation of the Spirit of Jesus—the living body of Christ on earth.

The Church as Body

Paul's metaphorical conception of the church as a body—the body of Christ—meant that the body torn at Calvary, buried, raised, and ascended back to the Father, had been replaced by the church. Individual members of the church formed the limbs, eyes, hands, and tongues of the body. Not only was the church a body in which Christ is the indwelling life, but Christ was also the ascended Head from whom "the whole body, joined and held together by every supporting ligament, grows and builds itself up in love, as each part does its work" (Ephesians 4:16).

An obvious truth emerges from Paul's conception of the church as the body of Christ. It is not possible to touch the lives of other Christians, for weal or woe, healing or comfort, without touching Christ as well.

In his great picture of the judgment in Matthew 25, Jesus warns that our treatment of others, for good or evil, and our treatment of him are synonymous. Jesus receives those on his right hand because, as he puts it, "I was hungry and you gave me something to eat, I was thirsty and you gave me something to drink, I was a stranger and you invited me in, I needed clothes and you clothed me, I was sick and you looked after me, I was in prison and you came to visit me" (Matthew 25:35-36).

When the righteous ask, "Lord, when did we see you hungry and feed you, or thirsty and give you something to drink? When did we see you a stranger and invite you in, or needing clothes and clothe you? When did we see you sick or in prison and go to visit you?" Jesus replies, "I tell you the truth, whatever you did for one of the least of these brothers of mine, you did for me" (Matthew 25:37-40).

Jesus rejects those on the left because, "I was hungry and you gave me nothing to eat, I was thirsty and you gave me nothing to drink, I was a stranger and you did not invite me in, I needed clothes and you did not clothe me, I was sick and in prison and you did not look after me" (Matthew 25:42-43).

When the unrighteous ask, "Lord, when did we see you hungry or thirsty or a stranger or needing clothes or sick or in prison, and did not help you?" Jesus answers, "I tell you the truth, whatever you did not do for one of the least of these, you did not do for me" (Matthew 25:44-45).

The Church as a Place of Caring

What are we to conclude from Jesus' teaching? Because the manner in which we treat our brothers is precisely the way we treat Christ, it is important that each one of us becomes his brother's keeper. Because it is impossible to love Christ sincerely without heartfelt interest in the welfare of other Christians, Paul commanded the Thessalonians to "encourage one another and build each other up" (1 Thessalonians 5:11).

When Peter considered the idea that our treatment of others is also our treatment of Christ, he instructed his readers to "live in harmony with one another; be sympathetic, love as brothers, be compassionate and humble. Do not repay evil with evil or insult with insult, but with blessing, because to this you were called so that you may inherit a blessing" (1 Peter 3:8-9).

For those who wonder how to make love for Christ come alive, Peter looks to Christian relationships and offers a list of practical pointers:

1. *Live in harmony with one another.* Believers must have one purpose and pleasure—to serve God and others.

2. *Be sympathetic.* Christians must not only understand the distress of others, but also must do all possible to relieve that distress.

3. *Love as brothers.* We must not speak disrespectfully of our brothers, lest we offend Christ. We must never take advantage of a fellow Christian, but make every effort to protect him and his interests.

4. *Be compassionate and humble.* Every Christian must understand that his brother is an individual that God created, not to be forced into some position of thought or action, but a being to appreciate and love.

5. *Do not repay evil with evil or insult with insult, but with blessing.* The temptation to strike back when someone treats us harshly is strong, but we must pour oil on troubled waters. We must go the second mile, and turn the other cheek. We must be gracious and winsome.

The Proof of our Love

It is impossible to be like Christ without genuine concern for the welfare of others. Although completely innocent, Jesus offered himself as a sacrifice for the good of others, including his enemies, becoming a ransom for the world. Jesus' sacrifice at Calvary was a perfect act of selfless love.

The prime test of our love for Christ is not how many hours we spend each day reading the scriptures, how many prayers we offer, or the frequency of our church attendance. The ultimate test of sincerity is our willingness to work unceasingly for the other person's highest good. The question on Judgment Day will not be, "How many Wednesday night prayer meetings did you attend?" The question will be, "How many needy saints did you attempt to help?"

If the church is the body of Christ of which we are members, it follows that the manner in which we treat others not only touches Christ, but ourselves as well. *The manner in which we treat others is precisely the way we treat ourselves, for we are members one of another—members of the same body.* To care for

lfare of others is therefore in our self-interest. The
t we become unconcerned about the life and health of
others in the body is the moment we begin to hasten our spiritual death.

I want to encourage you to take care of others. If you find it difficult to serve others at first, don't give up. Practice makes perfect. In time you will know the indescribable joy of being your brother's keeper.

Questions for Discussion

1. Why is the church a spiritual necessity?
2. List some passages from the Bible that say the church is a family.
3. In what sense is the church a family?
4. Why do we need the fellowship of other Christians?
5. How does the New Testament use the word "fellowship?"
6. In what sense is our treatment of the church also our treatment of Christ?
7. Why is it important to build up one another?
8. What does the New Testament picture of the church as the body of Christ imply about Christian relationships?
9. How do we make our love for Christ come alive?
10. Why is it impossible to be like Christ without concern for others?

Questions for Discussion

> "Live not as though there were a thousand years ahead of you. Fate is at your elbow; make yourself good while life and power are still yours."
> —Marcus Aurelius

Number 10

Resolve Anger Quickly

Woody Hayes coached football at Ohio State University for twenty-eight years. Besides winning football games, another trademark of Coach Hayes' career was his violent outbursts of temper. After almost three decades of extraordinary accomplishments, Ohio State University fired Woody Hayes for assaulting an opposing player during a game. With millions of others, I saw that game on television. A profound sense of sorrow overcame college football fans all over America. A single act of aggression would bring a brilliant football-coaching career to an end.

Unfortunately, Hayes, a hardworking man of honorable character, and loved by those close to him, remained all his life at the mercy of a demon called "anger." "When we lose a game," he once said, "nobody's madder at me than me. When I look into the mirror in the morning, I want to take a swing at me." I recall reading somewhere that after a loss to Iowa in 1963, Hayes made a bloody mess of his face with a large ring on his left hand.

Outbursts of anger usually lead to negative consequences. It cost Woody Hayes the opportunity to coach football at Ohio State. Who of us has not been embarrassed because we allowed our anger to explode? Besides embarrassment, our unbridled anger destroys friendships, damages relationships, destroys marriages, induces guilt, injures children, and makes of life a bit of hell on earth. Headlines of any local newspaper in America depict a world gone berserk on rage and resentment.

Anger and The Church

Besides the anger of the world, Christians sometimes bristle and fume in their own unique brew of venom and vindictiveness. You hear so many stories about fractured churches that you get the impression that every church is in one of three stages. Either it has just finished a fight, is in the middle of a fight, or getting ready for one.

Unfortunately, many churches are fertile soil for the seeds of discord. Conflicting ideas germinate, grow, and compete for survival. A live or die orientation destroys the fellowship of Christians, and makes of the church a place for the survival of the fittest. The battle rages. We fight one another fiercely. The stakes are high and the competition is relentless. No opposing view is too trivial for wars of debate. A win or lose mentality demands that any competing idea, no matter how insignificant, must be attacked with a brutality somewhat akin to Armageddon. So we set out to kill mosquitoes with cannon fire, unaware of how absurd we appear to outsiders who think primarily of Christianity as a religion of love.

Anger in the Bible

When we think of anger we usually assume that it includes aggressive behavior, but the scriptures distinguish between anger and aggression. From the Old Testament we learn that God was often angry. Anger also had an effect on the prophets. When Moses came down from the mountain where God gave him the commandments, and found the Israelites reveling in idolatry, he smashed the stone tablets that contained the law.

While the Bible distinguishes between anger and aggression, condemning only the aggressive behavior caused by anger, but not anger itself, it also teaches that anger is extremely dangerous.

It may be true that anger and aggression are different, but it is also true that there is an almost inevitable connection between the two. The scriptures therefore call upon us to resolve our anger quickly. Jesus said,

> You have heard that it was said to the people long ago, 'Do not murder, and anyone who murders will be subject to judgment.' But I tell you that anyone who is angry with his brother will be subject to judgment. Again, anyone who says to his brother, 'Raca,' is answerable to the Sanhedrin. But anyone who says, 'You fool!' will be in danger of the fire of hell. "Therefore, if you are offering your gift at the altar and there remember that your brother has something against you, leave your gift there in front of the altar. First go and be reconciled to your brother; then come and offer your gift. Settle matters quickly with your adversary who is taking you to court. Do it while you are still with him on the way, or he may hand you over to the judge, and the judge may hand you over to the officer, and you may be thrown into prison. I tell you the truth, you will not get out until you have paid the last penny (Matthew 5:21-26).

Paul gives similar advice when he says, "Therefore each of you must put off falsehood and speak truthfully to his neighbor, for we are members of one body. In your anger do not sin: Do not let the sun go down while you are still angry" (Ephesians 4:23-24). Because of the almost unavoidable linkage between anger and aggression, the apostle also encourages us to resolve our anger quickly.

This raises an important question. How will we solve, quickly and effectively, an emotion so turbulent as anger? It is one thing to know that it is important to resolve today's anger before sundown, and another to know how to do the task. One is easy. The other is difficult.

Passivity

If we are to solve anger quickly and effectively, it is imperative that we learn to make the proper response. Some react to anger with *passivity*. The person who deals with his anger passively is nonassertive. Because he never stands up for himself, others choose for him. He is indirect and self-denying, but he is also emotionally dishonest. He often denies that he ever has feelings of hostility, yet, in the end, he becomes irritated because he did not speak for himself when others violated his rights.

During my years of ministry and counseling, I have seen dozens of people whose lives were almost destroyed by hidden anger. Among my clients have been wives whose husbands were domineering and abusive. Because they thought it best not to cause trouble, they quietly accepted mistreatment. Lack of communication, consideration and respect, over a period of years, brutalized and angered some of them almost beyond help. Yet they were so passive that they never mentioned their pain. Strangely, some were so passive that they either did not know they were angry, or they denied it. They sought help only after the pain of anger became so intolerable that they could no longer refrain from admitting disgust with their passivity. Because of self-denial, their marriages were now in trouble. It would have been better to deal with the problem at the start.

I have counseled husbands and fathers who allowed annoyances with their wives and children to stew for years. Yet they never said a word about their anger. One man ended his marriage of twenty-five years because his wife refused to spend within the limits of the family budget. His wife lacked respect for the value of money. It disturbed him that there was so little family savings, that there was so little laid by for the years of retirement. So after twenty-five years of passivity, he suddenly exploded, venting too much anger too late.

Aggression

While some are passive, others respond to anger with *aggression*. They stand up for themselves, but they violate the other person. They are domineering, direct, superior, self-righteous, vengeful, and often out of control.

I am always shocked by news coverage of a gunman who walks into a public place and opens fire. Some are killed. Others are wounded. Often the gunman kills himself. When I hear such stories, I always ask, "Why didn't the shooter kill himself first?" My question assumes that the gunman either planned to take his life, or knew that he would be killed, so why didn't he commit suicide first, and spare the lives of innocent people?

I must conclude that the kind of behavior that makes one want to commit suicide, and take as many others with him as possible, finds its explanation in the kind of anger that resolves itself by aggression. This kind of thinking is not only criminal, but also maniacal. Obviously, aggression is not the proper way to deal with anger.

Constructive Response

The Christian way to deal with anger is with honest communication. The person who resolves anger constructively stands up for himself in a way that does not violate the rights of others. He levels with others, is expressive and direct, but he avoids hurting others. He respects himself, and is self-confident, but never self-righteous.

Jesus' behavior at the cleansing of the temple is a perfect example of how to resolve anger constructively. Jesus knew the purpose of the temple. He respected the temple as a place of prayer and worship. When greed made of the temple a place of merchandise, when dishonest money changers robbed worshipers by demanding an exorbitant rate of exchange, when evil men made a din of thieves of a place of prayer, Jesus' underlying annoyance suddenly surfaced. He responded to a violation of essential values by expressing his anger in a practical or useful way. Jesus knew when to get angry, and what to get angry about. In a positive way he expressed his indignation. To believe that Jesus went about thrashing men and animals with wild, passionate snorting is to read too much into the scripture's account of the temple cleansing. Unquestionably, Jesus was angry, but he did not sin. He did level with those whose actions caused his irritation. He gave the reasons for his frustration and anger, but he did not choose for others, and I suspect that very soon after Jesus left the scene, the money changers returned to set up shop again.

A friend of mine recently told a story that illustrates the power of dealing with anger quickly and constructively. When his son obtained a driver's license, he asked to use the family car on weekends. The young man took good care of the car, avoided trouble, and delivered it for his father's use every Monday morning in one piece. The only problem was that the gas tank was always empty. Every Monday morning for several weeks my friend limped to the nearest gas station on the wings of a prayer that the car would not stop in the middle of some busy intersection. It became too much to bear. One morning, limping, praying, hoping against hope that the car would not stall, my friend became furious.

My first inclination would be to deal with the problem by making a quick decision to deny the son further use of the car. "That will teach him not to bring home a car empty of gas," I would say. What my friend did was to have a meeting with his son in which he said, "Look, I love you, and I want you to enjoy the car on weekends, but I am very angry with you for always running the gas out of the car, and bringing it home empty. Unless you become more responsible you can no longer drive the car. You don't have to answer me now. Think about it for a few days, and let me know what you want to do."

A few days later, the young man told his father that he would be more responsible. The car never came home empty of gas again. It isn't surprising that the young man became a responsible, productive member of society. His life reflects his good upbringing by parents who, though angered often, dealt with their anger quickly and effectively.

Conclusion

Let's go back now to the question I asked at the beginning. How can we deal quickly and effectively with an emotion so powerful as anger? We must begin dealing constructively with our anger today. Like Jesus, we must level with others. We must be direct, expressive, and self-confident, without hurting others. We must speak kindly. Once we have had our say, we must let anger go.

Dealing constructively with anger also means that we must distinguish between the things worthy of resentment and those that are unworthy. As Aristotle put it, "It is easy to fly into a passion—anybody can do that—but to be angry with the right person to the right extent and at the right time and with the right object and in the right way—that is not easy, and it is not everyone who can do it."

Maybe Aristotle was right. Perhaps not everyone can do it. But Jesus did, and so must we. Jesus seldom became angry. When he did, his anger either burned toward the self-righteous, hypocritical Pharisees who prevented honest God-seekers from entering the kingdom, or he found those who desecrated holy things, and those who made merchandise of others, intolerable. With these few exceptions, Jesus was never angry. Incredibly, he even remained silent as he witnessed the ugliness of those who gave him a mock trial and sentenced him to death on a cross.

Clearly, Jesus became angry only at the violation of essential values. Like Jesus, we must learn how to become angry at the right time, to the right extent, for the right reasons, and with the right people.

Above all, when we become irritated, for whatever reason, let us resolve our anger before sundown that day.

Questions for Discussion

1. Discuss some negative consequences of anger.

2. What is wrong with the win or lose mentality that divides churches?

3. How may we solve, quickly and effectively, an emotion so turbulent as anger?

4. What is wrong with being passive toward those who anger us?

5. Why is it wrong to react aggressively toward those who anger us?

6. Is there a constructive way to deal with anger? How?

7. How did Jesus deal with anger?

8. Explain how it is possible to be angry without sinning.

9. Discuss Jesus' annoyance at the temple with the money-changers. How does Jesus' example help us deal positively with anger?

10. Discuss ways that make it possible for us to be angry with the right person to the right extent and in the right way?

"You can accomplish by kindness
what you cannot do by force."
—Publilius Syrus

Number 11

Be Humble toward One Another

It is often said of preachers that they exaggerate. I confess to overstatement of a problem in this chapter. Most wealthy, gifted, privileged and intelligent Christians are not egotistical or proud. Only a very few are unable to show humility toward others. Still, there is a need for the message of this chapter. If I overstate the case, or if I appear too dramatic, I can only say that the peace and harmony of the church is at risk because of a few self-absorbed people. I offer these warnings in the belief that most people are well intentioned, that they love others, and will make adjustments in attitude when encouraged to make positive changes.

Although power is the antithesis of Christianity, some believers have always pursued it. Even Jesus' disciples hungered for power. Several times during the final week of Christ's life they argued about who was best, and who would be first in the kingdom. Incredibly, in the very shadow of the cross, some of the disciples attempted to position themselves for power.

Somehow the disciples failed to grasp the importance of Jesus' warning in Luke 20:46-47:

Beware of the teachers of the law. They like to walk around in flowing robes and love to be greeted in the marketplaces and have the most important seats in the synagogues and the places of honor at banquets. They devour widows' houses and for a show make lengthy prayers. Such men will be punished most severely.

Jesus warned against the kind of thinking that caused the teachers of the law to seek power. With luxurious clothing, pious language, and lengthy prayers, they sought for special treatment, recognition, and seats of honor. While they attained positions of power, they also received severe punishment.

Jesus wanted the disciples to understand that the Christian life is a life, not of power, but of dependence. In his beatitudes, Jesus established that it is the powerless—the poor, the sorrowful, the meek, the pure, the peacemakers, the persecuted—who receive great reward.

Our Lord also gave many models that stood in stark contrast to those who sought power. There is a widow who lost her only son. With nothing left, she got the Lord's full attention and sympathy. Another widow gave all that she had, which wasn't much, to the temple treasury. Yet Jesus praised her as the most liberal giver that day—a day on which many wealthy worshipers made large contributions. There is the poor sinner who went to the temple to pray. Not even lifting his eyes toward heaven, he struck his breast with his clenched fists, and cried, "Oh God, be merciful to me a sinner." Unlike the Pharisee who could boast to God of his spiritual attainments, this poor sinner could plead only God's mercy. Yet he went home forgiven, whereas the Pharisee, with all his supposed spiritual assets, remained in sin.

Anonymity, Not Visibility

Clearly, Jesus commanded us to strive for anonymity, not visibility. Yet we struggle for power. Christian leaders often feel that the use of power helps them get things done. They have big dreams of building a great church, a great university, or they want to promote some private scheme, special ministry, or some organization or institution that they think will benefit mankind and glorify God. Unfortunately, those who pursue power to attain their dreams of greatness seldom pause to consider that reflected credit is their true motivation. They want to say, "Look at what I have done." Because it is easy to equate perceived God-given tasks with personal goals or dreams, power becomes a mandate from God. That others are used, even abused, in the attainment of personal glory is therefore acceptable to the power seeker because he can rationalize his mistreatment of others with the thought that he has done God's work. The end justifies the means.

All this is in sharp contrast to Jesus who was uninterested in securing his space, striving for power, and acquiring possessions. Contrary to the advice of those who know how to get and use power, Jesus demands selfless behavior. He says,

> But I tell you who hear me: Love your enemies, do good to those who hate you, bless those who curse you, pray for those who mistreat you. If someone strikes you on one cheek, turn to him the other also. If someone takes your cloak, do not stop him from taking your tunic. Give to everyone who asks you, and if anyone takes what belongs to you, do not demand it back (Luke 6:27-30).

While these words of Jesus may seem impractical to many modern disciples, the Lord plainly expounds the virtues of powerlessness, and owing to the Lord's total lack of concern for power, it is a bit astonishing that so many of his followers are skilled in its acquisition and use.

Power Plays

The wealthy, for example, sometimes use their money as leverage to cause policy changes in the local church. They know that the church must meet its budget or lose all. Thus the threat of withholding substantial contributions is a sure means of forcing others to acquiesce to their demands.

Wealth is power in another way. While there are many Christians who are both wealthy and sincere, there are some that use their wealth as power to force others into an acceptance of their supposed superior spiritual position. They point to their extravagant lifestyles, expensive trappings, and unique privileges as proof that God has singled them out for special love and recognition that others do not enjoy. This is a play for power at its worst, and best, for it nearly always works. How can you argue with a power seeker when he says that God is responsible for his elevated position in the world? Besides, such people intimidate us. Who will buy the argument that it is shameful to equate wealth with wisdom and power? Who will trade fame and fortune for the agony of commitment and self-denial? It is difficult, in a materialistic society, to admit that Christ died a hard death on an ugly cross—that the essence of Christianity is not power, but powerlessness.

Name-dropping is another power game some play. It makes an average person seem important if he knows famous and beautiful people who are Christians. This kind of power seeker allows only the brightest, the best-looking, the wealthiest, and the most sophisticated into his circle of friends. He knows who has the best inside information, who confides in whom, and he plays golf, tennis, or whatever the fad, only with the "right" people. Unlike Jesus, who himself was a loser in human terms, this kind of power seeker never associates with the poor, the maimed, and the weak. His abilities may be limited, but he attains credit and power by association with the right people. His undeserved, but lofty position makes it easy for him to manipulate others. He accepts praise for a job well done when others do the work. Others get the chores while he gets the cheers.

Besides all that, the power seeker often makes great use of pietistic language. How is it possible to answer the popular television evangelist who recently said, "The Lord told me that my ministry is the only ministry anointed by the Holy Ghost?" No one wants to argue with the Holy Spirit. Then, there are those who preface their opinions with phrases like: "Having searched the scriptures carefully for several years I think . . .." "I've spent many hours praying about this . . .." "I only have the best interest of everybody in mind . . .." The opinions of such people usually prevail because there is no easy way for others, whose judgment may be better, to answer their hallowed language.

Sadly, the lust for power reaches into the highest levels of church leadership. Someone on a church staff, for example, may pursue power by securing for himself the best place and space. He demands a large corner office because large corner offices are where power always resides. His furniture must be lavish, becoming a person of authority. One Christian leader studied how to arrange his office furniture in a manner to intimidate or catch others off guard. He also requires special secretarial help, a larger salary than others, and a special title. "Minister of Preaching," for example, seems more authoritative than the title, "Involvement Minister" or "Education Minister."

All this, of course, creates a problem for others that seek power, and who occupy hall offices and have less important sounding titles. Their problem is to find a way to make room for themselves at the top by displacing the occupant of the large corner office. They begin by cultivating the friendship of certain influential families of the congregation. In subtle ways, at first, they create doubt about the character and judgment of the one who seems to hold the reigns of power. Sometimes the criticism is that the one in power is a bit lazy or disorganized. Consequently some of those in corner offices are dislodged, and the power structure changes. Sadly, the whole process then begins anew.

Those who doubt that the use of power appeals to church workers should visit their libraries. Books by self-image advocates line their shelves. In subtle, perhaps unconscious ways, such books advise them to find fulfillment by taking charge of life. Sounds good! But the problem is that the gospel is not a self-help message.

There are those who train church leaders to develop their skills in creative confrontation, marketing, how to reach opinion makers, and how to attain a distinctive personality. They tell us that we will get to the top and stay there only if we succeed in challenging our detractors head-on with pizzazz and imagination. The problem I have with such advice is that it doesn't seem Christ-like.

My situation is unique. It happens that I reside in a corner office, have the title, "Minister of Preaching," and also serve as an elder. Wow! Some might view such a position as one of limitless power, for it combines the symbols of power with the perceived right to legislate or rule.

Elders often make the serious mistake of thinking that their office endows them with authority to rule. For that reason, churches appoint new elders with great difficulty. Many churches have had the heartbreaking experience of suggesting names for additional elders, only to have those prospective leaders denied the opportunity to serve. The new men are not acceptable to those already in authority because they might change the power structure. The existing group must not compromise its control by allowing others, with unpredictable ideas, the opportunity to effect changes of policy or direction. The present group must maintain the integrity of its authority because it leaves them with exclusive power to rule.

Power and Authority

The problem with such thinking is that *power* and *authority* are not synonymous. Power is seized. Authority is accepted. A despot has power, but the duly elected official of a democratic state has authority. Power is the coercion of unwilling people who, far from acknowledging a ruler's authority, submit for fear of the consequences. Power is forcing others to do what one wants for no other reason than he wants it. Authority, on the other hand, cannot always make its will effective. A police officer has the authority to clear the scene of a crime of spectators, but curiosity usually gets its way. What is a police officer to do with those who refuse to disperse? Shoot them?

Closely related to the idea of authority are things like competence, recognition, being in charge, and accountability. Again the police officer illustrates the point. He has the authority to protect society from criminals who would victimize innocent people, but if he becomes incompetent or ruthless, he must appear before his peers to answer charges of police brutality. Authority is always answerable to those who give it.

Only in the Godhead do we find the existence of both power and authority in one entity. For that reason, no one, except God, may legitimately rule the church. Elders, ministers, teachers, deacons—all Christians who lead—have authority, not power. They are accountable both to God and those they serve.

Even God, who has all power and authority, does not force others to do anything against their will. Obedience to God is always an individual decision. Nature may obey the laws of God without choice, but man may choose to disobey God. If God does not force his will on others, how can his people justify the use of power?

Reject the Use of Power

It may be difficult, but Christians must say no to power. We must reject the kind of thinking that says we cannot attain great goals without forcing our agenda on others. We must not accept the kind of reasoning that says the church doesn't work without power. We must follow the example of Jesus who, when tempted with power, rejected Satan's offer of "all the kingdoms of the world and their splendor" (Matthew 4:8-10).

Not only was Jesus himself powerless, but his ministry was to the powerless. He took as his purpose the words of Isaiah:

> The Spirit of the Sovereign LORD is on me, because the LORD has anointed me to preach good news to the poor. He has sent me to bind up the brokenhearted, to proclaim freedom for the captives and release from darkness for the prisoners, to proclaim the year of the Lord's favor and the day of vengeance of our God, to comfort all who mourn, and provide for those who grieve in Zion—to bestow on them a crown of beauty instead of ashes, the oil of gladness instead of mourning, and a garment of praise instead of a spirit of despair. They will be called oaks of righteousness, a planting of the LORD for the display of his splendor (Isaiah 61:1-3).

Because Jesus lacked concern about securing his place and space, his followers are under obligation to refrain from forcing their will on others. Living up to that obligation will not be easy. Many of us play the power game consciously, but others, perhaps most of us, have become so efficient in the acquisition and use of power that we go along unconsciously. For many of us, using power is like breathing—we do it automatically, even in our sleep. Each of us must therefore do some soul-searching to discover the ways we use power. Then with God's help. We must change. Let us be humble toward one another.

Questions for Discussion

1. Why is power the antithesis of Christianity?
2. How do Jesus' beatitudes prove that the Christian religion is a religion of dependence, not power?
3. Why should the Christian strive for anonymity, not visibility?
4. Why do you think so many Christians feel power is necessary?
5. Do you agree that Jesus was uninterested in power? Why?
6. What are some power games Christians play?
7. What is the difference between power and authority?
8. Why does God not force us to obey him?
9. Is it wrong for Christians to use power if they use it unconsciously? Why?
10. Why is it difficult for Christians to resist the use of power?

Number 12

Christian Freedom Is Mature and Responsible

A friend called for an appointment to meet at my office. He is thirty-something, energetic, and gifted. During a two-hour conversation I learned that he is unhappy with the church he attends because it has a rule that those who pray, make announcements, or serve communion, must "dress suitably for the occasion." Suitable dress means a coat and tie. My friend is irked by a rule that disallows his participation in the activities of the church assembly unless he dresses "to conform to middle-class expectations of divine worship." He holds firmly to an opinion that we have an obligation to wear "casual clothes" during Sunday services to show that worship is a part of "everyday" life. His justification for choosing another church is a feeling that the he is not free.

I sympathize with my friend. There is nothing wrong with reading the scriptures, praying, or even preaching a sermon, in casual clothes. I suspect that the first-century Christians seldom "dressed up" for their predawn assemblies in the caves and tombs where they met secretly to avoid persecution.

My friend also makes a good point when he says that the poor would feel more comfortable in our assemblies if we did not look so prosperous. As it is, the very people who need our help most—the poor, the diseased, the ugly—feel awkward and out of place in our churches.

Because we have liberty in Christ, freedom to dress for worship in casual clothes is allowable. That means, of course, that one is also free to wear a jacket and tie if he likes. Herein lies the problem. My friend complains that he wants to be free of arbitrary dress codes (he actually wants a rule that favors only casual attire in the assembly), while others argue that they have freedom to regulate. Whose opinion is right? Both have neglected the principle of mutual subjection. The ideal thing would be to allow those who wish to do so, to wear formal clothing and those who don't wish to wear formal attire should be allowed to participate in the assembly in casual clothing.

We must learn, however, that Christian freedom never embodies the right to do exactly what we like with no regard for the well being of others. Those who argue their freedom in Christ, without regard for others, are like the prisoner who sees the door of his cell open, and runs out at top speed without pausing to think about where he will get his next meal, or how he will make it in a world of other free people. Freedom must be mature and responsible.

All Things Are Lawful

When I say that Christians must be mature and responsible, I in no way intend to convey the meaning that our liberty in Christ has constraints. In matters of opinion, freedom in Christ has absolutely no limits or restrictions. Paul says four times that everything is lawful (1 Corinthians 6:12; 10:23). There is no specific Christian way of life that imposes a set way of thinking about manners, ideas, procedures, attitudes, or opinions. Christians have the freedom to hold different, even contradictory opinions if they wish. Paul says in Romans 14, for example that we may or may not eat meat offered to idols. We may or may not recognize special days as having religious significance. He writes,

> One man considers one day more sacred than another; another man considers every day alike. Each one should be fully convinced in his own mind. He who regards one day as special, does so to the Lord. He who eats meat, eats to the Lord, for he gives thanks to God; and he who abstains, does so to the

Lord and gives thanks to God. For none of us lives to himself alone and none of us dies to himself alone. If we live, we live to the Lord; and if we die, we die to the Lord. So, whether we live or die, we belong to the Lord (Romans 14:5-8).

The Christian may marry or remain single. He may be a conscientious objector or a soldier like Cornelius. He may be wealthy or take a vow of poverty. He may dress elegantly for church attendance or wear everyday clothes. He may sing contemporary music in praise of God or he may sing traditional hymns. I prefer traditional hymns, with a sprinkling of contemporary songs. One may feel that only cathedral-like church buildings give glory and honor to God, or he may worship in a simple structure to show the proper scorn for the world's riches. Absolutely any lifestyle can be a legitimate expression of one's freedom in Christ. In matters of taste, temperament, and opinion, we decide how we should serve God.

If one is reckless, he has the freedom even to contend with God. One may fling questions at God like Job. He may spurn God like Jonah who angrily refused to go to Nineveh, or Moses who refused to go to Pharaoh. He may, like Elijah, even accuse God of forsaking him. If man has freedom to refuse and accuse God, how can anyone deny that all things are lawful or allowable for him?

All Things Are Lawful, But . . ..

While it is true that all things are lawful, not all things are helpful. Paul wrote, "Everything is permissible—but not everything is constructive. Nobody should seek his own good, but the good of others" (1 Corinthians 10:23-24).

The context of the passage in 1 Corinthians 10 is a discussion about eating meat sacrificed to idols. Paul is both free and not free. It is permissible for him to eat meat, but it is not beneficial if in eating he wounds, shocks, or destroys a brother. The apostle may not hurt his brother needlessly. A brother must be built up, and forcing a personal opinion will make the task impossible. The apostle makes the same point in his letter to Rome when he says,

Therefore let us stop passing judgment on one another. Instead, make up your mind not to put any stumbling block or obstacle in your brother's way. As one who is in the Lord Jesus, I am fully convinced that no food is unclean in itself. But if anyone regards something as unclean, then for him it is unclean. If your brother is distressed because of what you eat, you are no longer acting in love. Do not by your eating destroy your brother for whom Christ died. Do not allow what you consider good to be spoken of as evil. For the kingdom of God is not a matter of eating and drinking, but of righteousness, peace and joy in the Holy Spirit, because anyone who serves Christ in this way is pleasing to God and approved by men.

Let us therefore make every effort to do what leads to peace and to mutual edification. Do not destroy the work of God for the sake of food. All food is clean, but it is wrong for a man to eat anything that causes someone else to stumble. It is better not to eat meat or drink wine or to do anything else that will cause your brother to fall (Romans 14:13-21).

Paul is free, but he must use his freedom to choose actions that benefit or edify a brother. Thus Christian freedom is never without direction and purpose. Its purpose is to choose acts that help others. Christian freedom never exploits others for some selfish end.

Freedom from Self

All this raises an important question. How can one be free when selfless concern for the welfare of others is the only possible motivation for action? The answer, obviously, is that Christian freedom is freedom from self to choose others. A Christian is nothing if not a person concerned primarily about the welfare of others. Christianity consists in never sacrificing a human being for any purpose or selfish desire.

Freedom from self-centeredness is the first step of true liberty in Christ. The one who insists on having his way, selfishly acknowledging that he has no obligations to others, confuses liberty with license. We are not free merely to be free—to do as we like—evading all responsibility to the welfare of others. We are free to love and serve others.

Because love chooses what is best for others, it provides freedom an opportunity to take shape. All talk of freedom apart from obligations to others is nonsense. Before God created Eve, Adam had no thoughts of freedom. A society of one feels no constraints or restrictions. Freedom is a sensible idea only within the framework of human relationships, and the highest expression of Christian freedom is to act voluntarily in the other person's best interest. Paul confirms all this when he says,

> Though I am free and belong to no man, I make myself a slave to everyone, to win as many as possible. To the Jews I became like a Jew, to win the Jews. To those under the law I became like one under the law (though I myself am not under the law), so as to win those under the law. To those not having the law I became like one not having the law (though I am not free from God's law but am under Christ's law), so as to win those not having the law. To the weak I became weak, to win the weak. I have become all things to all men so that by all possible means I might save some. I do all this for the sake of the gospel, that I may share in its blessings (1 Corinthians 9:19-23).

Paul became all things to all men because his concern for others compelled a course of behavior that was beneficial to them. The apostle exercised his freedom to adopt any lifestyle necessary to help him win the lost. He could be Jew or Gentile, extravagant or thrifty, flamboyant or subdued, cerebral or practical—all things to all men that he might by "all possible means" win some.

Those who feel that Paul's actions are hypocritical do not understand the compelling power of a love that is never for ideas, opinions, social standing, race, class or status, but for people. We see that kind of love at Calvary. At the cross we learn that the more one loves people, the more compelled he is to choose actions that promote their good. So the apostle adopted the attitudes and feelings of others. He temporarily embraced inconsequential lifestyles and opinions so that he might meet men on their ground.

Conclusion

Clearly, we may not separate Christian freedom and responsibility. Christianity is not a matter of confirming oneself in isolation from others, but a matter of self-affirmation in relation to a brotherhood. We are not "pious particles," but "members of one another." The Christian exists not for himself, but to empty himself for the sake of others. Since Christ gave his life in service to us, how can we do less for his people? God has placed us in the world to be instruments of his reconciling mission. Whatever else being a Christian means, it surely includes helping our brothers and sisters claim all that their birthright gives them.

Questions for Discussion

1. If we must be in subjection to others, how can we be free in Christ?

2. What does Paul mean when he says, "All things are lawful, but not all things are helpful?

3. How may Christians hold differing, even contradictory opinions, and maintain unity?

4. In what sense is the Christian both free and not free (1 Corinthians 10:23-24)?

5. What is the relationship between freedom and responsibility? Between freedom and love?

6. Why is freedom from self the first step to liberty in Christ?

7. Why was Paul not hypocritical when be became "all things to all men?"

8. Why is freedom a sensible idea only within the framework of human relationships?

9. Explain the difference between liberty and license.

10. Why does freedom from all responsibility to the body of believers result in spiritual death?

"When you are kind to someone in trouble,
you hope they'll remember and be kind
to someone else. And it'll become like a wildfire."
—Whoopi Goldberg

Number 13

Build Up One Another

In chapter six I argued that because the command for us to love one another occurs so often in the scriptures, and because Jesus said that love is the greatest command, we must conclude that other commands of the scriptures, although important, are not as weighty as our obligation to love one another. This chapter makes a similar argument for the principle of mutual subordination and edification.

Although every truth in the scripture is both valuable and needed, not every truth of the scripture is equally important. Jesus called upon the lawyers and Pharisees to identify matters that were most significant when he said,

> Woe to you, teachers of the law and Pharisees, you hypocrites! You give a tenth of your spices—mint, dill and cummin. But you have neglected the more important matters of the law— justice, mercy and faithfulness. You should have practiced the latter, without neglecting the former (Matthew 23:23).

When asked what he thought was the greatest command, Jesus quoted from the Old Testament, "Love the Lord your God with all your heart and with all your soul and with all your strength and with all your mind; and, love your neighbor as yourself" (Luke 10:27).

Paul, too, thought some truths of the scripture were more important than other truths were. For example, the apostle identified the resurrection of Christ as the most important fact of the gospel he preached. Concerning the resurrection, he said to the Corinthians,

> For what I received I passed on to you as of first importance: that Christ died for our sins according to the Scriptures, that he was buried, that he was raised on the third day according to the Scriptures, and that he appeared to Peter, and then to the Twelve (1 Corinthians 15:3-5).

Clearly, both Jesus and Paul rejected a level view of the scripture that sees every passage as of equal value and consequence. Jesus knew that love for God is the only sufficient motivation for a lifetime of obedience.

A Procedure for Priority

This raises some important questions. If all scriptures are not of equal weight and consequence, how are we to know what is most important? May we make arbitrary choices about what ideas of the scripture are more important than others are? Doesn't the view that some passages are more important than others open the way for the naïve or deceitful to lead the church astray?

Obviously, the decision about what scriptures are most important cannot be left to the individual to work out as he pleases. God, alone, decides what is most valuable. We know, for example, that it is more important to display justice, mercy, and faithfulness, than to tithe, because Jesus made that claim. Because Jesus said it, we know also that the greatest command is to love God. The resurrection of Christ is a matter of "first importance" because Paul proclaimed its significance. In other words, we decide what the most important scriptures are by basing our conclusions on apostolic statements, and not on our feelings or personal interests.

Another way to decide the importance of a teaching of the scripture is to notice the number of times it recurs. A truth oft repeated is very important.

The Center of Christianity

Because of the torrent of scriptures in the New Testament that use the phrase "one another," we must conclude that concern for others is the quintessence of Christianity. More passages explain our obligations to one another than speak of baptism, the Lord's Supper, and numerous other subjects that captivate our thinking and admiration. The following passages, for example, impress us with the importance of being our brother's keepers:

A new command I give you: *Love one another.* As I have loved you, so you must *love one another* (John 13:34).

By this all men will know that you are my disciples, if *you love one another* (John 13:35).

Be devoted to one another in brotherly love. *Honor one another* above yourselves (Romans 12:10).

Live in harmony with one another. Do not be proud, but be willing to associate with people of low position. Do not be conceited (Romans 12:16).

Let no debt remain outstanding, except the continuing debt to *love one another*, for he who loves his fellowman has fulfilled the law (Romans 13:8).

Therefore *let us stop passing judgment on one another.* Instead, make up your mind not to put any stumbling block or obstacle in your brother's way (Romans 14:13).

Accept one another, then, just as Christ accepted you, in order to bring praise to God (Romans 15:7).

I myself am convinced, my brothers, that you yourselves are full of goodness, complete in knowledge and competent to *instruct one another* (Romans 15:14).

Greet one another with a holy kiss. All the churches of Christ send greetings (Romans 16:16).

I appeal to you, brothers, in the name of our Lord Jesus Christ, that all of you *agree with one another* so that there may be no divisions among you and that you may be perfectly united in mind and thought (1 Corinthians 1:10).

All the brothers here send you greetings. *Greet one another with a holy kiss* (1 Corinthians 16:20).

Greet one another with a holy kiss (2 Corinthians 13:12).

You, my brothers, were called to be free. But do not use your freedom to indulge the sinful nature; rather, *serve one another in love* (Galatians 5:13).

Be kind and compassionate to one another, forgiving each other, just as in Christ God forgave you (Ephesians 4:32).

Speak to one another with psalms, hymns and spiritual songs. Sing and make music in your heart to the Lord (Ephesians 5:19).

Submit to one another out of reverence for Christ (Ephesians 5:21).

Bear with each other and *forgive whatever grievances you may have against one another.* Forgive as the Lord forgave you (Colossians 3:13).

Let the word of Christ dwell in you richly as you *teach and admonish one another* with all wisdom, and as you sing psalms, hymns and spiritual songs with gratitude in your hearts to God (Colossians 3:16).

Therefore *encourage one another* and build each other up, just as in fact you are doing (1 Thessalonians 5:11).

But *encourage one another daily,* as long as it is called Today, so that none of you may be hardened by sin's deceitfulness (Hebrews 3:13).

And let us consider how we may *spur one another on toward love and good deeds* (Hebrews 10:24).

Let us not give up meeting together, as some are in the habit of doing, but let us *encourage one another*—and all the more as you see the Day approaching (Hebrews 10:25).

Brothers, *do not slander one another.* Anyone who speaks against his brother or judges him speaks against the law and judges it. When you judge the law, you are not keeping it, but sitting in judgment on it (James 4:11).

Now that you have purified yourselves by obeying the truth so that you have sincere love for your brothers, *love one another deeply, from the heart* (1 Peter 1:22).

Finally, all of you, *live in harmony with one another;* be sympathetic, love as brothers, be compassionate and humble (1 Peter 3:8).

Offer hospitality to one another without grumbling (1 Peter 4:9).

Young men, in the same way be submissive to those who are older. All of you, *clothe yourselves with humility toward one another,* because, "God opposes the proud but gives grace to the humble" (1 Peter 5:5).

Greet one another with a kiss of love. Peace to all of you who are in Christ (1 Peter 5:14).

This is the message you heard from the beginning: We should *love one another* (1 John 3:11).

And this is his command: to believe in the name of his Son, Jesus Christ, and *to love one another* as he commanded us (1 John 3:23).

Dear friends, let us *love one another,* for love comes from God. Everyone who loves has been born of God and knows God (1 John 4:7).

Dear friends, since God so loved us, we also ought to *love one another* (1 John 4:11).

No one has ever seen God; but if we *love one another,* God lives in us and his love is made complete in us (1 John 4:12).

And now, dear lady, I am not writing you a new command but one we have had from the beginning. I ask that *we love one another* (2 John 1:5).

A Matter of Life or Death

Such a deluge of scriptures overwhelms us. How can we be Christians without caring for others? The Christian individualist who boasts of his freedom in Christ argues against the inevitable. Just as it is the nature of planks to float and pebbles to sink, so the distinctiveness of Christianity is its service to others. The only possible response to the flood of scriptures is to imitate Jesus who wrapped himself in a towel and washed the dirty feet of his disciples.

Some things are life or death matters. To cross the sea without a compass, to walk across a desert without necessary provisions, or to jump from an airplane without a parachute, is to commit suicide. Because living for others is the Christian's guiding star, selfishness leads to darkness and spiritual death. Only by following his star, can the Christian find purpose now and Heaven's safe harbor later.

Christians who cannot be helpers and partners of others walk in darkness, not in light. An anonymous writer described the impoverished state of a selfish, self-centered Christian when he wrote,

I was hungry
And you formed a humanities club.
Thank you.

I was naked
And in your mind
You debated the morality of my
Appearance.

I was homeless
And you preached to me
Of the spiritual shelter of the
Love of God.

I was imprisoned
And you crept off quietly
To your chapel in the cellar
And prayed for my release.

I was sick
And you knelt and thanked God for
Your health.

I was lonely
And you left me alone
To pray for me.

Conclusion

A clear truth emerges. If the church is to be the family of Christ on earth—a place where people feel loved and alive, we must refuse to be masters, and become servants of others. We must not stress the importance of our interests only, but wait patiently upon others. Instead of holding hard for our personal rules and opinions, we must become sympathetic and reasonable. We must cease living by a schedule to which others must conform, and begin to sacrifice graciously as others need us. We must cease making friends only with the lovable, and we must begin loving the unlovable and forgiving the seeming unforgivable.

Questions for Discussion

1. Explain why some scriptures are more important than others.

2. Why did Jesus say that love for God is the greatest of all commands?

3. Why did Paul say that the resurrection was the most important truth of the gospel?

4. Why are justice, mercy, and faithfulness more important than tithing?

5. How do we know which scriptures are the most important?

6. How many passages in the New International Version use the phrase, "one another"? How many occur in the King James Version? What do so many scriptures imply?

7. Why is selfishness the antithesis of Christianity?

8. Why is service to others the essence of Christianity?

9. How do we make others feel loved?

10. How is it possible to love the unlovable and forgive the seeming unforgivable?